INTRODUCTION

Dieting with Asian food has many pluses—you can lose weight on a healthy, low-fat diet that offers tremendous variety, texture and flavour.

Asian meals, however, often don't include dessert, so if you crave something sweeter than fruit, remind yourself of those extra kilojoules before you splurge!

NOTES

• These recipes serve 6 people.

• Those on a diet should only eat a 90 g portion of chicken or meat and ½ cup of rice or noodles (or as recommended by their dietitian or doctor). Vegetables are very low in kilojoules, so no limit is placed on these. Those not on a diet can consume larger portions—the important thing is that the dishes are still intrinsically healthy. Always have a balanced meal—soup, a meat, vegetables or salad, and rice or noodles. Some dishes that include rice or noodles as an ingredient are a meal in one dish.

• Some Asian dishes are sweetened with a small amount of sugar. However, when divided among the number of servings per dish, the kilojoule count is negligible.

• The amount of oil used in recipes has been reduced to the equivalent of 1 teaspoon or less per serving.

• Some dishes contain desiccated coconut or coconut milk. Coconut is high in saturated fat, but once more the amount has been reduced so that the coconut flavour is retained without the worry of a high kilojoule count.

Desiccated coconut has about double the kilojoule count of freshly grated coconut. Both have been used in small amounts but, if desired, they can be omitted. One tablespoon of desiccated coconut contains 170 kilojoules; again, when this is divided between 6 portions the extra kilojoule count per serving is very small.

- Canned coconut milk/cream products vary slightly in kilojoule count, but on average ¼ cup contains about 500 kilojoules which, when divided between 6 servings, gives only 80 kilojoules per person. Do not confuse canned coconut milk made from the flesh of the coconut with the clear liquid which comes from inside a fresh coconut (¼ cup has only about 45 kilojoules).

- Creamed coconut is yet another product. This is usually found in the form of a solid block and may be added directly or diluted with hot water. In solid form its kilojoule count is about ⅓ as high again as that of canned coconut milk. I don't recommend its use by anyone trying to slim!

- Flavourings and thickenings such as soy sauce, fish sauce, plum sauce and cornflour are added in such small amounts that they will not increase kilojoule counts to any great degree.

- To prevent vegetables burning when frying in a reduced amount of oil use a heavy based pan and fry at a lower heat, stirring frequently. Alternatively, use a non-stick pan. Wok frying works well with a small amount of oil since the food is constantly tossed and is cooked for a very short time. If vegetables do stick to the base of the pan add a little hot water and stir.

- Before cooking, cut all visible fat off meat and discard the skin and internal fat from chicken. Some cuts of chicken, notably the thighs, have small pockets of fat which are visible once the bone has been removed. Take a little time to remove these.

HEALTHY

ASIAN

Ealir
& W

rsmith

wlc.ac.uk

CHARMAINE SOLOMO

HAMLYN

Published 1993 by Hamlyn
an imprint of the Octopus Publishing Group,
a division of Reed International Books Australia Pty Ltd
22 Salmon Street, Port Melbourne, Victoria 3207

Designed by Louise Lavarack
Photographs by Michael Cook
Styling by Margaret Alcock
Food cooked by Nina Harris, Jill Pavey, Tim McFarlane Reid
China: 'Foglia' by Villeroy & Boch
Ceramic bowls from Made in Japan, Neutral Bay, NSW
Typeset in 9½ on 12pt Berkeley Old Style Book by Midland Typesetters
Produced in Hong Kong by Mandarin Offset

National Library of Australia
 cataloguing-in-publication data:

Solomon, Charmaine.
 Healthy Asian food.
 Includes index.
 ISBN 0 947334 48 3.

 1. Cookery, Oriental. 2. Nutrition. I. Title. (Series: Solomon,
 Charmaine. Asian cooking library).

641.595

Soups

Asian soups are seldom served as a first course. Usually they are a liquid accompaniment to the meal or, in some cases, a complete meal in themselves. For the dieter, however, it is probably best to start with a soup as it will take the edge off the appetite and prevent over-indulging in the more substantial food which follows.

The velvety texture created by the very finely chopped chicken breast gives this soup its name.

Chicken Velvet Soup

- 500 g (1 lb) chicken breast fillets
- ½ teaspoon salt
- 3 egg whites
- 7 cups Chinese Chicken Stock (see p. 10)
- 375 g (12 oz) canned creamed corn
- 2 tablespoons cornflour
- 1 teaspoon sesame oil
- 1 tablespoon dry sherry
- 2 thin slices lean smoked ham, finely chopped

Chop chicken very finely until almost puréed or use food processor. Add salt and 3 tablespoons cold water; mix well. Beat egg whites until frothy and fold into chicken purée. Reserve.

In a saucepan bring chicken stock to boil; stir in corn. Mix cornflour with ¼ cup cold water. Bring stock mixture back to boil and stir in cornflour. Return to boil, stirring until thickened. Stir in sesame oil, sherry and reserved chicken. Simmer, stirring, for 2 to 3 minutes. Serve immediately sprinkled with ham.

Thai Chicken and Noodle Soup

- 6 cups Chinese Chicken Stock (see p. 10)
- 1 whole chicken breast, skin removed
- 125 g (4 oz) rice vermicelli
- 2 teaspoons Pepper and Coriander Paste (see below)
- 2 teaspoons fish sauce
- 1 cup fresh bean sprouts
- ½ cup sliced spring onions
- 1 or 2 red or green chillies, sliced and seeded
- coriander leaves to garnish

Heat stock in a large saucepan; add chicken breast to pan and simmer very gently for 6 to 8 minutes. Turn off heat and leave chicken to cool in liquid. Remove chicken from stock and discard bones. With a sharp knife cut flesh into neat slices. Soak rice vermicelli in hot water for 10 minutes.

Reheat stock and stir in Pepper and Coriander Paste, fish sauce, bean sprouts and spring onions. Drain rice vermicelli and add to pan. Heat through, stir in chicken slices and serve garnished with chilli slices and coriander leaves.

Pepper and Coriander Paste
A really useful paste to have on hand since it contains flavourings basic to Thai cooking.
Makes about 1 cup

- 1 tablespoon chopped garlic
- 2 teaspoons salt
- 2 tablespoons whole black peppercorns
- 2 cups well-washed, coarsely chopped fresh coriander, including stems and roots
- 2 tablespoons lemon juice

Crush garlic with salt to a smooth paste. Roast peppercorns in a dry pan for 1 to 2 minutes, then crush coarsely in a mortar and pestle. Finely chop coriander. Mix all ingredients with lemon juice. (You can make this paste in a blender, but reduce the peppercorns to 1 tablespoon, since the more finely ground the hotter they are!) Store in the refrigerator in a clean glass jar.

A fairly thick soup with a pronounced sour and spicy flavour.

LENTIL AND VEGETABLE SOUP

- *1 cup split peas or red lentils*
- *1 tablespoon tamarind pulp or 1 teaspoon instant tamarind*
- *1 tablespoon oil*
- *1 tablespoon ground coriander*
- *2 teaspoons ground cummin*
- *¼ teaspoon ground black pepper*
- *½ teaspoon ground turmeric*
- *⅛ teaspoon asafoetida, optional*
- *3 cups mixed vegetables (zucchini, eggplants, beans, pumpkin— cut into bite-size pieces)*
- *2 fresh green chillies, seeded and sliced*
- *½ teaspoon black mustard seeds*
- *1 small onion, finely sliced*
- *salt to taste*

Wash split peas or lentils well. If using peas soak for at least 2 hours. Drain and simmer in 6 cups water until soft. Soak tamarind pulp in 1 cup hot water for 5 minutes and squeeze to dissolve pulp. Strain, discarding seeds and fibres (or dissolve instant tamarind in hot water). Add liquid to lentils.

In another heavy saucepan heat 2 teaspoons of oil and fry ground spices and asafoetida over very low heat, stirring, for 1 to 2 minutes. Pour lentil mixture into this pan; add vegetables and chillies and simmer until vegetables are cooked.

Heat remaining oil in a small, heavy frying pan and fry mustard seeds and onion until seeds pop and onion is brown. Stir frequently so that onion does not burn. Stir into soup, salt to taste, simmer a few minutes longer and serve as a first course or with steamed rice.

Note If tamarind is difficult to obtain, lime or lemon juice can be substituted. Use enough to give a distinctly tart flavour.

A mild Thai vegetable soup flavoured with dried shrimp.

Mixed Vegetable Soup

- *⅓ cup dried shrimp*
- *5 fresh coriander roots*
- *1 large clove garlic, chopped*
- *1 teaspoon dried shrimp paste*
- *¾ cup chopped onions*
- *5 cups Chinese Chicken Stock (see p. 10)*
- *4 cups vegetables such as bamboo shoot, beans, straw mushrooms, baby corn cobs, zucchini and broccoli, sliced into bite-size pieces*
- *2 tablespoons fish sauce*
- *1 teaspoon palm sugar or brown sugar*
- *½ cup basil or coriander leaves*

Soak dried shrimp in hot water to cover for 10 minutes. Drain; place in a blender or food processor with coriander roots, garlic, shrimp paste and onions. Add a little water if necessary and blend to a purée.

Add purée to stock and bring to boil. Add vegetables, putting in those which require longer cooking first. Stir in fish sauce and sugar and toss in basil or coriander leaves at the last minute. Serve hot.

Pea Soup with Coconut

- ¾ cup split peas
- ½ teaspoon ground turmeric
- salt to taste
- 1 tablespoon tamarind pulp or 1 teaspoon instant tamarind
- 1 teaspoon brown sugar
- 2 teaspoons oil
- ½ teaspoon black mustard seeds
- sprig of fresh curry leaves or 10 dried curry leaves
- 2 fresh green chillies, seeded and chopped
- 1 fresh red chilli, seeded and chopped
- 2 cloves garlic, finely chopped

Wash split peas well and soak in water for 2 hours. Drain and place in a saucepan with turmeric and 8 cups water. Bring to boil; cover and cook until peas are very soft—about 1 hour. (If mixture becomes too thick before peas are cooked, add more water.) Add salt to taste. Soak tamarind pulp in 1 cup hot water for 5 minutes, then squeeze to dissolve pulp; strain liquid into hot pea mixture (or mix instant tamarind with hot water until dissolved). Add sugar.

In a heavy based pan, heat oil and fry mustard seeds, curry leaves and chillies over low heat, stirring constantly until mustard seeds pop. Add garlic and cook 1 minute more. Pour mixture into soup, stir well and simmer for another 5 minutes. This dish can be served as a soup or with steamed rice.

- *2 tablespoons desiccated coconut*
- *1 tablespoon chopped fresh coriander*

Toast coconut in a dry pan, stirring constantly until browned. Turn onto paper towel to cool. Serve coconut and chopped coriander in small, separate bowls, to be added as desired.

A thin soup from South India which is served as a digestive, either spooned over rice or taken at the end of a meal.

Pepper Water

- *1 tablespoon tamarind pulp*
- *2 large cloves garlic, sliced*
- *½ teaspoon ground black pepper*
- *1 teaspoon ground cummin*
- *salt to taste*
- *2 tablespoons chopped fresh coriander*
- *1 teaspoon oil*
- *1 teaspoon black mustard seeds*
- *sprig of fresh curry leaves or 10 dried curry leaves*

Soak tamarind pulp in 1 cup hot water for 5 minutes, then squeeze to dissolve pulp. Strain, discarding seeds and fibres. Place tamarind liquid, garlic, pepper, cummin, salt and coriander in a saucepan with 4 cups cold water and bring to boil. Reduce heat immediately and simmer for 10 minutes.

Heat oil in a small heavy based pan and fry mustard seeds and curry leaves, stirring, until leaves brown. Add to simmering soup and serve.

A Vietnamese combination that is a dieter's dream—the strongly flavoured stock is combined with other fresh, low-fat ingredients, making a complete meal in a bowl.

BEEF SOUP WITH SALAD

- 3 kg (6 lb) beef rib bones
- 500 g (1 lb) shin beef
- 2 onions, chopped
- 1 tablespoon sliced fresh ginger
- 1 small stick cinnamon
- 1 teaspoon whole black peppercorns
- salt to taste
- 500 g (1 lb) fresh bean sprouts
- 4 firm ripe tomatoes halved, then sliced
- 500 g (1 lb) rump steak or fillet
- 6 spring onions, sliced thinly
- 2 white onions, sliced thinly
- 500 g (1 lb) fresh rice noodles or 250g (8 oz) dried rice noodles
- fish sauce
- lemon wedges
- fresh red or green chillies, chopped and seeded
- fresh coriander leaves, chopped

Put bones and shin beef in a stockpot or very large saucepan. Add plenty of cold water to cover and onions, ginger, cinnamon, and peppercorns. Bring to boil, reduce heat to very low, cover and simmer for at least 4 hours. Add salt to taste.

Pinch off straggly ends of bean sprouts. Place sprouts in a colander and pour boiling water over. Rinse under cold water, drain and place in serving bowl. Trim fat from steak and slice, paper thin, into bite-size pieces. (This is easier if meat is partially frozen.) Arrange tomatoes, steak, spring and white onions on serving plate.

If using fresh noodles, slice into 1 cm (½ inch) strips, pour boiling water over, then drain. (For dried noodles: cook noodles in boiling water 6 to 8 minutes, until just tender. Drain well.) Transfer noodles to serving bowl.

When ready to serve, place fish sauce, lemon wedges, chillies and coriander leaves in small bowls on the table. Remove shin beef from strained stock and cut into bite-size pieces. Return to pot. Place stock in a heating utensil at the table.

Each diner puts a serving of noodles and bean sprouts into their own large soup bowl, then puts a few slices of beef, tomato and onion into a large ladle and immerses it in boiling stock until beef turns pale pink. Pour contents of the ladle over the noodles and sprouts. Fish sauce, lemon juice, chillies and coriander leaves are added to suit individual taste.

LENTIL MULLIGATAWNY

- *1 cup red lentils*
- *2 medium onions*
- *1 clove garlic, chopped*
- *1 small stick cinnamon*
- *½ teaspoon whole black peppercorns*
- *1 teaspoon oil*
- *sprig of fresh curry leaves or 10 dried curry leaves*
- *salt to taste*
- *½ teaspoon garam masala*
- *¼ cup canned coconut milk*

Wash lentils well and leave to soak for about 1 hour. Drain and place in saucepan with 1 onion, garlic, cinnamon and peppercorns. Add 6 cups water and bring to boil. Cover and simmer until lentils and onion are soft. Force through a sieve to make a purée, discarding spices.

Finely slice remaining onion. Heat oil in saucepan and fry onion and curry leaves, stirring, until onion is brown. Add lentil purée, salt and garam masala; simmer for 2 minutes.

Mix coconut milk with ¾ cup water and add to soup, stirring until heated through.

*One of those soups which can be an entire meal. In this case,
it will make 3 servings rather than 6.*

COMBINATION LONG SOUP

- 6 dried shiitake (Chinese) mushrooms
- 2 eggs, beaten
- salt and pepper to taste
- few drops sesame oil
- 250 g (8 oz) fine egg noodles
- 8 cups Chinese Chicken Stock (see p. 10)
- 3 teaspoons peanut oil
- 1 clove garlic, peeled and bruised
- 2 slices fresh ginger
- 250 g (8 oz) lean pork or chicken, finely shredded
- 3 cups white Chinese cabbage, cut in strips
- 1 canned bamboo shoot, diced
- 2 tablespoons light soy sauce
- 1 tablespoon dry sherry
- ½ teaspoon sesame oil

Soak mushrooms in hot water to cover for 30 minutes. Remove
and discard stems and slice caps finely. Season eggs with a
little salt and pepper. Lightly grease a heated omelette pan
with a few drops of sesame oil. Pour in enough beaten egg
to make a thin omelette. Repeat with remaining egg. Slice
omelettes finely and set aside.

Cook noodles for 2 minutes in a large pot of boiling water. (If the noodles are in tight bundles, soak in warm water first for 10 minutes to separate strands and ensure even cooking. Lift out on a slotted spoon and drop into boiling water.) Drain in colander and rinse with cold water to separate. Drain again. Heat chicken stock.

Meanwhile heat peanut oil in a wok; stir-fry garlic and ginger, discarding when brown. Add pork or chicken to wok and fry quickly, stirring, until colour changes. Add cabbage and bamboo shoot and stir-fry 2 minutes more.

Add noodles and fried mixture to chicken stock. Return to boil. Add soy sauce, sherry and salt to taste. Stir in sesame oil and serve immediately, garnished with omelette strips.

Usually a flavour base for soups, served alone it makes an ideal dieter's chicken broth. Serve sprinkled with a few chopped coriander leaves or finely sliced spring onions. It is also suitable for use in Thai soup recipes.

CHINESE CHICKEN STOCK

- 1 kg (2 lb) chicken bones, including neck and feet
- 10 black peppercorns
- 2 small stalks celery with leaves
- 1 onion
- few stalks fresh coriander, including root
- 2 thick slices fresh ginger
- salt to taste

Place chicken bones in a saucepan with 8 cups cold water and remaining ingredients. Bring to boil, skimming if necessary. Cover and simmer for 45 minutes to 1 hour. Strain and chill. Any fat will congeal on surface and can be easily removed.

CHICKEN AND BEAN CURD SOUR SOUP

- 185 g (6 oz) cooked chicken (skin and bones removed)
- 185 g (6 oz) firm bean curd
- 6 dried shiitake (Chinese) mushrooms
- 185 g (6 oz) bamboo shoot, or celery stalk
- 90 g (3 oz) snow peas
- 6 cups Chinese Chicken Stock (see p. 10)
- 3 tablespoons rice vinegar or white wine vinegar
- 1 teaspoon black pepper, freshly ground
- 1½ tablespoons light soy sauce
- 1 large egg, lightly beaten

Dice chicken and bean curd. Soak mushrooms in hot water to cover for 30 minutes, remove stems and discard. Slice caps into thin strips. Cut bamboo shoot or celery stalk into julienne strips. Remove strings from snow peas and slice diagonally into 2 or 3 pieces. Bring stock to boil and add chicken, bean curd, mushrooms and bamboo shoot or celery and simmer for 3 to 4 minutes. Add snow peas, vinegar and pepper and simmer 1 minute more. Whisk soy sauce into beaten egg. Increase heat under pan and pour in beaten egg and soy sauce in a steady stream. Serve immediately.

A Japanese dish served in soup bowls with a dipping sauce. You can substitute other varieties of seafood or vegetables. Make Dipping Sauce ahead of time and cool.

Simmered Seafood and Vegetables

- 500 g (1 lb) snapper or bream fillets
- 1 lobster tail
- 1 cup cooked and drained bean thread vermicelli
- 8 cups dashi (use dried or liquid instant dashi and follow instructions on label)
- 2 small carrots, sliced
- small piece kombu (Japanese dried kelp)
- soy sauce to taste
- 100 g (3½ oz) fresh mushrooms, sliced
- 6 spring onions, cut into bite-size lengths

Wash fish and cut into 2.5 cm (1 inch) pieces. With a sharp cleaver cut lobster tail into slices. Cut vermicelli into short lengths. Place in a saucepan with dashi and bring to boil. Reduce heat and simmer for 5 minutes; add carrots, kombu and soy sauce. Simmer 2 minutes more. Add fish and lobster and simmer for 5 minutes or until ingredients are just cooked. Add mushrooms and spring onions during the last 1 to 2 minutes. Serve in soup bowls accompanied by small, individual dishes of Dipping Sauce. The ingredients are eaten with chopsticks and dipped in the Sauce as desired. The soup is drunk from the bowl.

Dipping Sauce

- 1 cup dashi
- ¼ cup Japanese soy sauce
- ¼ cup mirin or dry sherry
- pinch salt or sugar

Put dashi, soy sauce and mirin in a small saucepan and bring to the boil. Remove from heat and cool. Add salt or sugar to taste.

Clear Soup with Pork and Bean Curd

- 150 g (5 oz) pork fillet
- 250 g (8 oz) firm bean curd
- 6 dried shiitake (Chinese) mushrooms
- 6 cups hot Chinese Chicken Stock (see p. 10)
- 5 spring onions, cut in 4 cm (2 inch) lengths
- 1 tablespoon grated ginger
- 1 tablespoon light soy sauce

Remove fat from pork and discard. Shred pork. Dice bean curd and set aside.

Soak mushrooms in hot water to cover for 30 minutes then remove stems and slice caps finely. Add pork and mushrooms to hot stock and simmer for 2 to 3 minutes. Add bean curd, spring onions and ginger juice (obtained by squeezing grated ginger between two spoons) with soy sauce. Serve immediately. Don't overcook ingredients or soup will lose its light, fresh taste.

Prawn Soup

- 60 g (2 oz) bean thread noodles
- 8 dried shiitake (Chinese) mushrooms
- 2 cloves garlic, finely chopped
- ½ cup chopped fresh coriander, including roots
- 375 g (12 oz) raw prawns
- 1 tablespoon peanut oil
- 1 onion, sliced finely
- 4 spring onions, sliced finely
- 2 tablespoons fish sauce
- 1 teaspoon sugar or to taste

Place noodles in a bowl and cover with boiling water. Leave to soak. Soak dried mushrooms in hot water to cover in a separate bowl for 30 minutes. Cut off stems and discard. Slice caps thinly. Drain noodles and cut into short lengths. Chop garlic and coriander together finely.

Shell and devein prawns. Heat half of oil, add shells and heads and stir-fry for a few minutes. Add 6 cups water and simmer for 20 minutes to make stock. Strain.

Heat remaining oil and fry onion over low heat, stirring frequently, until soft. Add garlic and coriander and fry, stirring until fragrant. Add prawns and fry until they change colour. Add hot stock, mushrooms and noodles. Simmer gently for 5 minutes. Stir in remaining ingredients.

Miso is a Japanese fermented soy bean paste which comes in different varieties according to the type of malt added. For the slimmer it is ideal, being low in kilojoules but satisfying and flavoursome at the same time. The miso is combined with dashi (a bonito fish stock) and tofu and/or different vegetable garnishes.

MISO SOUP

- *1 small leek*
- *12 button mushrooms*
- *6 cups dashi (use dried or liquid instant dashi and follow instructions on label)*
- *3 tablespoons miso*

Wash leek well and slice across into thin rounds. Wipe mushroom caps, trim stems and cut mushrooms across in thin slices. Bring dashi to boil in a saucepan. Put miso into a ladle and immerse the ladle slowly into broth, stirring constantly with chopsticks until miso dissolves (or dissolve in a small bowl using a spoon if you prefer). Stir dissolved miso gradually into pot, making sure there are no lumps. Add leek and mushrooms. As soon as broth boils again, remove from heat—it is important not to overcook the miso since overcooking destroys its aroma.

An attractive Thai soup in which the stuffed cucumbers look like flower buds. Use Chinese Chicken Stock (see p. 10) for this dish.

Soup with Stuffed Cucumbers

Soup
- 6 cups chicken stock
- 2 kaffir lime leaves, fresh or dried
- 1 teaspoon sugar, or to taste
- 1 clove garlic, crushed
- 1 tablespoon fish sauce
- 2 tablespoons lime juice
- 1 teaspoon Hot and Sour Soup Paste (see p. 17)

Place all soup ingredients in a large stainless steel or enamel saucepan and simmer, covered for 20 minutes.

Carefully place Stuffed Cucumbers in soup liquid, base downwards, and simmer gently for 8 to 10 minutes, just until pork is cooked.

Stuffed Cucumbers
- 2 small green cucumbers
- 125 g (4 oz) finely minced lean pork
- 2 teaspoons fish sauce
- 1 small clove garlic, crushed
- pinch ground black pepper
- 1 strip lime rind, finely chopped

Cut cucumbers crosswise into short lengths. With a sharp knife shape one end like the petals of a flower. Scoop out some of the seeds with a small spoon, leaving sufficient to form base of cup. Combine remaining ingredients, mixing well. Form into small balls and place one in each cucumber cup.

A teaspoon of this flavouring will give an exciting piquancy to a simple chicken broth. Use it to flavour other dishes too.
Makes about 1½ cups. Store in a glass jar in refrigerator.

HOT AND SOUR SOUP PASTE

- ½ cup dried shrimp
- ½ cup finely sliced lemon grass
- 1 tablespoon finely chopped garlic
- 2 tablespoons chopped coriander roots
- 10 whole peppercorns
- 1 tablespoon galangal, finely chopped
  or 2 teaspoons dried galangal powder
- 4 fresh red chillies
- 4 fresh green chillies
- 8 kaffir lime leaves, fresh or frozen
- 4 tablespoons fish sauce
- 4 tablespoons lime juice
- ½ cup vegetable oil
- 2 teaspoons chilli powder
- 1 teaspoon ground turmeric
- 1 tablespoon dried shrimp paste
- 1 tablespoon salt
- 1 tablespoon sugar
- 1 tablespoon citric acid
- 1 teaspoon finely grated lime rind

Process dried shrimp in a blender or food processor until it reduces to a floss. Transfer to a bowl.

Purée lemon grass, garlic, coriander, peppercorns, galangal, chillies and kaffir lime leaves in food processor or blender with fish sauce and lime juice. Place oil in a warm wok or heavy frying pan and cook chilli powder, mixed with 1 tablespoon water, stirring over low heat, until oil turns red.

Add puréed mixture with turmeric, shrimp paste and shrimp floss. Cook, stirring until oil comes to the surface. Transfer to a bowl and cool. Stir in salt, sugar, citric acid and lime rind.

You can buy soup paste, but by making it you can be sure it contains no monosodium glutamate or other additives.

SEAFOOD

Low in kilojoules and high in protein, fish is the ideal food for health-conscious weight watchers.

Ideal treatment for those dark-fleshed, oily fish which need strong flavours rather than delicate seasoning.

PIQUANT FISH CURRY

- 1 kg (2 lb) fish steaks or fillets
- 1 tablespoon dried tamarind or 1 teaspoon instant tamarind
- 1 tablespoon vegetable oil
- 2 teaspoons black mustard seeds
- ½ teaspoon fenugreek seeds
- 1 large onion, finely chopped
- 1 tablespoon finely chopped garlic
- 1 tablespoon finely grated fresh ginger
- 1 teaspoon ground turmeric
- 2 teaspoons ground cumin
- salt to taste

Rinse and dry fish on paper towel. Cut into serving pieces and set aside. Soak dried tamarind in 1½ cups hot water for 5 minutes, squeeze to dissolve pulp. Strain, discarding seeds and fibre. (Alternatively dissolve instant tamarind in water.)

Heat oil in a heavy saucepan and fry mustard seeds until they pop. Add fenugreek seeds, onion, garlic, and ginger and fry over low heat, stirring, until onion is soft and golden. Add turmeric and cumin and stir for 1 minute. Then add salt and tamarind liquid. Bring to boil, add fish and simmer over low heat until fish is cooked.

FISH STEAMED IN BANANA LEAVES

- 1 kg (2 lb) white fish fillets
- 1 large lemon
- 3 medium onions
- 1½ teaspoons finely chopped fresh ginger
- 3 cloves garlic
- 3 large fresh green chillies, seeded and chopped
- 1 cup fresh coriander leaves
- 2 teaspoons ground cummin
- ¼ cup fresh grated or desiccated coconut
- 2 teaspoons vegetable oil
- salt to taste
- 1 teaspoon garam masala
- banana leaves or foil

Rinse fish and dry with paper towels. Peel lemon, removing white pith. Cut in pieces, discarding pips. Place in blender or food processor with 2 onions, roughly chopped, ginger, garlic, chillies, coriander leaves and cummin. Process until puréed, then add coconut and blend again.

Finely chop remaining onion and fry in oil over low heat, stirring frequently, until soft and golden. Add puréed mixture and fry, stirring, until fragrant. Remove from heat and stir in salt and garam masala. Coat each fillet with mixture. Wrap in squares of banana leaf or foil (if using banana leaves, wash and dry first) and steam parcels on a rack over gently simmering water for 30 minutes, covered. Serve in the parcels. Place a bowl on the table to collect the discarded leaves or foil.

You will need to buy fillets which can be cut into good sized cubes for this dish. Firm-fleshed fish such as snapper, ling, jewfish and gemfish are ideal.

SPICED FISH KEBABS

- *1 kg (2 lb) firm, white fish fillets*
- *2 teaspoons grated fresh ginger*
- *3 cloves garlic, crushed*
- *salt to taste*
- *1 tablespoon ground coriander*
- *1 teaspoon garam masala*
- *½ teaspoon chilli powder*
- *1 tablespoon lemon juice*
- *1 cup low-fat plain yoghurt*
- *2 teaspoons plain (all-purpose) flour*

Rinse fillets and dry on paper towel. Cut into 4 cm (1½ inch) pieces. Place remaining ingredients in a large bowl and mix well. Add fish pieces and fold in gently until each piece is coated with marinade. Leave for 15 minutes at room temperature or longer in the refrigerator. Thread fish on bamboo skewers, about 4 or 5 on each, ensuring that the skin on each piece of fish is on one side of the skewer. (Soak skewers in water before use to prevent them burning under the griller.)

Place kebabs on an oiled tray under a preheated griller and cook 10 cm (4 inch) away from heat with skin upwards for 4 minutes. Turn skewers and grill other side for 4 to 5 minutes, depending on thickness of fish. Be careful not to overcook. Serve immediately accompanied by rice or chapatis.

FISH CURRY WITH TOMATO

- 750 g (1½ lb) fish fillets
- 2 teaspoons oil
- 1 large onion, finely chopped
- 3 cloves garlic, finely chopped
- 3 tablespoons chopped fresh mint leaves
- 1½ teaspoons ground cummin
- 1½ teaspoons ground turmeric
- 1 teaspoon chilli powder or to taste
- 2 large ripe tomatoes, chopped
- 1 teaspoon salt or to taste
- 2 teaspoons garam masala
- lemon juice to taste

Wash fish and cut into serving pieces. Heat oil in a heavy saucepan over very low heat and fry onion, stirring, until it becomes soft and transparent. Add garlic and mint; cook, stirring, until onion is golden. (It is important to keep heat low and to stir frequently as, with a reduced amount of oil, onion will burn more easily.)

Add cummin, turmeric, and chilli powder and stir until spices are aromatic. Stir in tomato, salt and garam masala; continue to cook and stir until tomato becomes a pulp. Add lemon juice. Place fish pieces in tomato mixture, spooning sauce over them. Cover and simmer for 10 minutes, or until fish is opaque. Serve with rice.

A Japanese delicacy of raw fish which has become increasingly popular in other countries. The fish must be impeccably fresh, its delicate flavour contrasting beautifully with the accompaniments of hot green horseradish paste and soy sauce.

SASHIMI
For each serving

- *125 g (4 oz) tuna, salmon, bream, bonito, kingfish, or jewfish*
- *1 tablespoon finely shredded giant white radish (daikon)*
- *1 tablespoon finely shredded carrot*
- *1 sprig of watercress*
- *1 teaspoon prepared green horseradish (wasabi—see Note)*
- *Japanese soy sauce*
- *mirin or dry sherry*

You may find some fish—such as tuna—especially prepared for sashimi and available at fish markets, but apart from these you should not buy fillets or any frozen fish for this dish. Purchase whole fish and have it filleted or fillet it yourself, removing all bones. Carefully cut away the skin.

With a sharp knife (and handling the fish as little as possible) cut fillet into thin slices and arrange on a serving plate. You can cut tuna and bonito in small cubes; other fish can be cut into bite-size slices and overlapped; small fish and squid can be cut into thin strips. Part of the appeal is in the artistic arrangement of the pieces.

Serve with shredded white radish and carrot and decorate with a sprig of watercress. Accompany each serving with a small mound of wasabi and an individual sauce dish holding Japanese soy sauce or a mixture of soy and mirin or sherry.

Note   Wasabi is a pungent green powder available in tins. It is reconstituted (like dry mustard) by the addition of a little cold water. Go easy: it is every bit as hot as English mustard. Also sold in tubes as a paste.

Since this is an acid-based curry, it is best to cook it in a non-aluminium pan.

FISH IN CHILLI TOMATO SAUCE

- *750 g (1½ lb) fish fillets*
- *3 tablespoons vinegar*
- *3 tablespoons fish sauce*
- *2 tablespoons hot chilli sauce*
- *3 teaspoons brown sugar*
- *1 tablespoon oil*
- *3 onions, chopped finely*
- *500 g (1 lb) ripe tomatoes, peeled, seeded and chopped*
- *1 sprig fresh coriander leaves*
- *2 or 3 red chillies, finely sliced and seeded*

Rinse fish and dry on paper towel. In a small bowl mix vinegar, fish sauce, chilli sauce and brown sugar, stirring to dissolve sugar.

Heat oil in a heavy based pan and fry onions over low heat, stirring frequently, until soft and beginning to turn golden. Add tomatoes and vinegar mixture, cover and simmer for 15 to 20 minutes until sauce is thick. Add fish fillets, spooning sauce over them. Cover and cook gently until fish is done. Do not overcook. Serve garnished with coriander leaves and sliced red chillies.

STEAMED FISH WITH TAMARIND AND GINGER

- *3 small whole fish*
- *coarse salt*
- *2 teaspoons finely grated fresh ginger*

Buy fish cleaned and scaled. Rub cavity with coarse salt to get rid of any blood. Rinse and blot dry. Score fish three or four times on each side. Rub inside and out with grated ginger mixed with a little salt. Place on a lightly oiled heatproof dish and steam for about 10 minutes or until flesh is opaque. Keep warm.

SAUCE
- *2 teaspoons peanut oil*
- *2 teaspoons finely chopped garlic*
- *1½ tablespoons shredded ginger*
- *6 spring onions, finely sliced*
- *1 teaspoon brown sugar*
- *1 tablespoon dried tamarind pulp (see Note)*
- *1½ tablespoons fish sauce*
- *2 teaspoons cornflour*
- *fresh coriander leaves*
- *red chilli strips*

Heat oil in a small saucepan over low heat and fry garlic for a few seconds, stirring. Add ginger and spring onions, frying for a few seconds longer until soft. Add sugar, tamarind liquid (see Note) and fish sauce. Bring to boil. Stir in cornflour mixed with 1 tablespoon cold water and as soon as Sauce clears and thickens, spoon over fish. Serve garnished with coriander leaves and chilli strips.

Note Soak tamarind in ¾ cup hot water for 10 minutes, squeeze to dissolve pulp, strain out seeds and fibres.

SPICED BAKED FISH

- *2 x 1 kg (2 lb) whole fish of choice*
- *salt*
- *lemon juice*
- *1 tablespoon oil*
- *2 tablespoons fresh ginger, finely chopped*
- *6 cloves garlic, finely chopped*
- *1 fresh red chilli, seeded and chopped*
- *1 fresh green chilli, seeded and chopped*
- *2 teaspoons ground cummin*
- *2 teaspoons garam masala*
- *2 cups low-fat plain yoghurt*
- *salt to taste*
- *fresh coriander leaves*

Purchase the fish cleaned and scaled. Rub inside of cavity with salt and rinse well. Dry fish and make diagonal slits in flesh on each side. Sprinkle a little lemon juice inside and into slits; set aside.

Heat oil in a heavy based frying pan and fry ginger, garlic and chillies over low heat, stirring frequently, until soft. Add cummin and garam masala and fry for 2 to 3 minutes more. Remove from heat, stir in yoghurt and add salt.

Line a baking dish with non-stick baking paper. Spread marinade over fish, and inside cavities. Leave to stand at room temperature for 30 minutes, then bake in a moderate oven for 35 minutes or until flesh is opaque at thickest part. Serve hot, garnished with coriander leaves.

STEAMED FISH WITH WALNUTS

- 6 x 300 g (10 oz) whole white fish
- salt
- 2 teaspoons finely grated fresh ginger
- ¼ cup light soy sauce
- ½ cup peeled walnuts (see Note)
- 2 teaspoons sesame oil
- 6 spring onions, thinly sliced

Purchase fish cleaned and scaled. Rub each cavity with salt and rinse. Trim fins and spines and score fish. Rub each fish inside and out with ginger and soy sauce. Place in a heatproof dish. Steam fish for 15 minutes, or until flesh is opaque when tested at thickest part.

Roast walnuts in a slow oven, 150°C, until pale golden, about 12 minutes.

When fish is cooked combine remaining soy sauce with sesame oil and pour over fish. Sprinkle with walnuts and spring onions.

Note   Peeled walnuts are available at Chinese stores and are preferable to ordinary walnuts because the skin can give a bitter taste. To peel them yourself, bring to the boil, drop into iced water until cold, then lift off skin with point of a toothpick or pin.

SPICED MUSSELS

- *1.5 kg (3 lbs) fresh mussels*
- *1 tablespoon oil*
- *3 onions, finely chopped*
- *6 cloves garlic, finely chopped*
- *1 tablespoon finely chopped fresh ginger*
- *3 fresh red chillies, seeded and chopped*
- *1 teaspoon ground turmeric*
- *1 tablespoon ground coriander*
- *2 tablespoons chopped coriander leaves*
- *lemon juice and salt to taste*

Scrub mussels well under running water and pull off beards. Do not use mussels with shells that are not tightly closed. Heat oil in a large, deep saucepan and fry onions, garlic, ginger and chillies over low heat, stirring frequently until onions are soft and golden. Add turmeric and coriander and stir for 3 minutes. Add 1 cup water, bring to boil and simmer, covered, for 5 minutes.

Add mussels. Cover pan and steam mussels for about 5 minutes, shaking pan from time to time, until shells have opened. (Some may open a little sooner than others: do not overcook, however, as they will become tough. Discard any mussels that do not open.) Remove from heat. Transfer mussels to a serving dish. Stir coriander leaves into sauce remaining in pan. Add lemon juice and salt to taste. Spoon sauce over and into mussel shells and serve immediately.

RED COOKED FISH

- 2 x 1 kg (2 lb) whole white fish
- 1 teaspoon salt
- 1 teaspoon five spice powder
- ¼ teaspoon black pepper
- ½ cup dark soy sauce
- ¼ cup dry sherry
- 2 teaspoons sesame oil
- 2 teaspoons sugar
- 6 thin slices fresh ginger
- 3 cloves garlic, bruised
- 2 whole star anise
- 4 spring onions, cut into short lengths
- 2 teaspoons cornflour
- spring onion flowers or sprigs of fresh coriander for garnish

Purchase fish cleaned and scaled. Wash fish and wipe dry with paper towels. Score fish lightly, making three or four diagonal slashes on each side. Combine salt, five spice powder and pepper. Rub mixture into slashes and cavities in fish. Combine soy sauce, sherry and sesame oil with 1½ cups water and stir in sugar until dissolved.

Place fish in a large pan or baking dish. Pour soy sauce mixture over. Add ginger, garlic, star anise and spring onions. Bring liquid to boil over medium heat, then lower heat so that liquid just simmers. Cover and cook for about 15 minutes, basting fish 2 or 3 times. Test at thickest part of fish with the point of a knife. If flesh is opaque and flakes easily, fish is ready.

Carefully lift fish onto a serving platter. Strain sauce left in pan. Heat 1 cup of sauce and stir in cornflour mixed with 1 tablespoon cold water. When sauce boils and thickens slightly, pour over fish and serve, garnished with spring onion flowers or sprigs of coriander.

Note You can store excess sauce in the freezer for other seafood dishes.

GARLIC SCALLOPS

- *500 g (1 lb) scallops*
- *1 tablespoon soy sauce*
- *1 tablespoon oyster sauce*
- *2 tablespoons dry sherry*
- *1 teaspoon cornflour*
- *3 teaspoons peanut oil*
- *1 small red capsicum, finely sliced*
- *3 large cloves garlic, finely chopped*
- *1 teaspoon sesame oil*
- *shredded lettuce to garnish*

Remove dark vein from scallops. Rinse and dry on paper towels. Mix soy sauce, oyster sauce, dry sherry and cornflour in a small bowl.

Heat wok, add peanut oil and heat again for 30 seconds. Add capsicum and stir-fry over medium heat for 1 minute. Add garlic and fry for a few seconds, stirring. Do not let garlic brown or it will taste bitter. Add scallops and stir-fry for 30 seconds. Pour in sauce mixture. Stir until sauce boils and thickens slightly: this will only take a few seconds. Remove from heat, sprinkle sesame oil over surface and mix. Serve immediately, garnished with shredded lettuce.

Note   Do not overcook scallops or they will shrink and become tough and leathery.

SZECHWAN-STYLE STIR-FRIED SQUID

- 750 g (1½ lbs) cleaned squid tubes
- large red capsicum
- ¾ cup chicken stock or water
- 1 teaspoon sugar
- salt to taste
- 1 teaspoon chilli oil
- 1 teaspoon cornflour
- 1½ tablespoons peanut oil
- 2 cloves garlic, finely chopped
- 8 spring onions (use some green tops), cut into bite-size pieces
- 1½ tablespoons preserved radish with chilli

Slit body of squid lengthwise. Rinse well and drain on paper towel. Slant knife at a 45° angle and make diagonal slits with a sharp knife on the inner surface, cutting first one way then the other to make a diamond pattern. Cut into 5 cm (2 inch) squares.

Remove seeds and cut capsicum into pieces. Combine stock with sugar, salt and chilli oil. In a separate small bowl mix cornflour with 1 tablespoon cold water. Heat peanut oil in a wok, swirling to coat, and when very hot add squid and stir-fry, tossing so that all surfaces are cooked. As soon as squid curls and becomes opaque, it is done. Overcooking will make it tough. Lift squid out with a slotted spoon.

Reheat wok, add capsicum, garlic, spring onion and radish and stir-fry over high heat for 1 minute.

Add stock mixture and, as soon as liquid comes to boil, mix in cornflour mixture and stir until it thickens slightly. This should take only a few seconds. Return squid to wok and toss well. Serve immediately with rice.

STIR-FRIED PRAWNS AND CHINESE GREENS

- 750 g large raw prawns
- 2 choy sum (Chinese vegetable) or gai choy (Chinese mustard cabbage)
- ¾ cup stock
- 2 tablespoons light soy sauce
- 1 teaspoon five spice powder
- ¼ cup dry sherry
- 2 teaspoons cornflour
- 1 tablespoon peanut oil
- 3 cloves garlic, crushed
- 2 teaspoons finely grated fresh ginger

Shell and devein prawns. Cut choy sum or gai choy into bite-size pieces, using the thick stems and only the tender part of the leaves. In a small bowl combine stock, soy sauce, five spice powder, and sherry. Mix cornflour with 2 tablespoons cold water.

Heat oil in wok. Add garlic, ginger and cabbage and fry for 2 minutes over high heat, stirring constantly. Add prawns and fry until pink.

Lower heat to medium, add mixed seasonings. Cover and simmer for 2 minutes. Add cornflour mixture and stir until sauce boils and thickens, about 1 minute. Serve at once.

CHICKEN
AND EGGS

ROAST SPICED CHICKEN

- 3 spatchcocks, about 500 g (1 lb) each
- ¾ teaspoon saffron strands
- 6 cloves garlic, peeled, finely chopped
- 1½ teaspoons salt
- 1½ tablespoons finely grated fresh ginger
- 2 tablespoons lemon juice
- 1 teaspoon chilli powder
- 2 teaspoons garam masala
- ¾ cup thick natural yoghurt
- 1 tablespoon oil

Remove skin from spatchcocks, slitting through skin front and back. Leave skin on wings (it is too difficult to try and remove it from these joints). Make slits in the flesh of the thighs, drumsticks and breast to allow spices to penetrate.

Toast saffron in a dry pan over gentle heat for a few seconds until dry and crisp, taking care strands do not burn. Turn onto a saucer and, when cool, crush with back of a spoon and dissolve in 2 tablespoons hot water. Combine with garlic, salt, ginger and lemon juice, chilli powder, garam masala and yoghurt.

Rub spice mixture over spatchcocks, especially in slits made in flesh. Cover and leave to marinate for at least 2 hours, or refrigerate overnight.

The best way to cook the birds is over a barbecue, first

letting the fire burn down to glowing coals. Cut spatchcocks in halves lengthways, place on a rack and cook until tender, turning with tongs.

If this is not possible, preheat oven to 200°C (400°F). Place spatchcocks, breast side down, in a roasting pan lined with lightly oiled foil or non-stick baking paper. Make sure birds are not touching. Brush backs lightly with oil. Roast in hot oven for 20 minutes, turn them over and continue roasting for a further 25 minutes or until done. If flesh appears to be drying out, cover pan loosely with foil. Serve hot, with flat bread and Onion and Coriander Salad (see p. 53).

Egg Curry

- *8 eggs*
- *1 tablespoon oil*
- *2 large onions, finely chopped*
- *4 cloves garlic, finely chopped*
- *1 tablespoon finely grated fresh ginger*
- *1 tablespoon ground coriander*
- *2 teaspoons ground cummin*
- *1 teaspoon ground turmeric*
- *½ teaspoon chilli powder*
- *3 large ripe tomatoes, diced*
- *salt to taste*
- *1 teaspoon garam masala*

Hard boil eggs and cool quickly in a bowl of cold water. Shell the eggs. Heat oil in a large, heavy based frying pan and fry onions, garlic and ginger over low heat, stirring frequently, until golden brown. Add ground spices and fry for a few seconds. Add tomatoes and salt, cover and cook until tomatoes are pulpy. Stir in 1 cup hot water; cover and simmer until mixture is thickened. Add garam masala. Slice eggs in halves lengthwise and carefully stir into sauce. Heat through and serve with rice or chapatis.

BARBECUED CHICKEN KEBABS

- *750 g (1½ lb) boned and skinned chicken thighs*
  - *1 large onion, roughly chopped*
    - *2 cloves garlic, peeled*
  - *1 tablespoon finely chopped fresh ginger*
    - *juice of 2 limes or 1 lemon*
    - *2 teaspoons ground coriander*
    - *½ teaspoon ground cummin*
    - *1 teaspoon garam masala*
    - *⅓ cup plain low-fat yoghurt*
    - *1 teaspoon salt or to taste*
  - *2 tablespoons chopped fresh mint leaves*

Remove any fat from chicken thighs and cut into bite-size pieces. Place onion, garlic, and ginger in food processor or blender and process until smooth, adding lime juice to facilitate mixing. Combine with ground spices, yoghurt, salt and mint leaves in a large bowl. Add chicken pieces and stir to coat.

Marinate chicken for 2 hours at room temperature, or refrigerate overnight if possible. Thread chicken pieces on bamboo skewers and cook over glowing coals or under a preheated griller until cooked through. (Don't forget to soak bamboo skewers in water before use to prevent them burning.) Serve with rice or chapatis.

KASHMIRI SAFFRON CHICKEN

- *1 tablespoon oil*
- *1 large onion, finely chopped*
- *4 cloves garlic, finely chopped*
- *2 teaspoons finely grated fresh ginger*
- *3 fresh red chillies, seeded and sliced*
- *½ teaspoon saffron strands*
- *¾ teaspoon ground cardamom*
- *1.5 kg (3 lb) prepared chicken pieces—breasts, thighs and drumsticks—skin removed*
- *salt to taste*

Heat oil in a heavy frying pan and gently fry onion, garlic, ginger and chillies, stirring frequently, until onion is soft and golden. Heat saffron in a dry pan over low heat—do not let it burn. Crush and dissolve in 2 tablespoons very hot water. Add to frying pan with cardamom and stir well. Add chicken and increase heat, turning chicken to coat with saffron mixture. Add salt to taste, cover and cook over moderate heat until chicken is tender. Uncover and cook until liquid is reduced.

POT ROASTED CHICKEN

- 1 x 1.8 kg (3½ lb) roasting chicken
- 1 large onion, roughly chopped
- 2 cloves garlic
- 2 fresh red chillies, seeded and chopped
- 3 teaspoons ground coriander
- 2 teaspoons ground cummin
- 1 teaspoon ground fennel
- 1 teaspoon ground turmeric
- 2 teaspoons chopped galangal in brine
- 1 teaspoon finely grated lime rind
- 1 tablespoon oil
- 1½ teaspoons salt or to taste
- 1 tablespoon lemon juice
- ½ cup canned coconut milk

Skin chicken and remove any fat from cavity. Wash well and dry inside and out with kitchen paper. Place onion, garlic, chillies, spices, galangal and lime rind in electric blender and blend to a smooth paste, adding a little water if necessary. Heat oil in a small pan and fry blended ingredients over low heat, stirring constantly, until mixture darkens and takes on an oily sheen. It should smell fragrant. Remove from heat and mix in salt and lemon juice.

Rub mixture inside and outside chicken. Mix coconut milk with 1½ cups water. Pour a little into the base of a deep, heavy ovenproof pot and place chicken in it, breast downwards. Pour remaining coconut milk mixture around chicken. Cover and roast in oven preheated to 180°C (350°F) for about 1½ hours or until cooked, basting every 20 minutes and turning chicken breast upwards halfway through cooking. Carve chicken and serve with coconut sauce.

SCRAMBLED EGGS, INDIAN STYLE

- *8 eggs*
- *⅓ cup low-fat milk*
- *salt to taste*
- *¼ teaspoon ground black pepper*
- *1 tablespoon oil*
- *6 spring onions, finely chopped*
- *3 fresh green chillies, seeded and chopped*
- *1 teaspoon finely grated fresh ginger*
- *3 tablespoons chopped fresh coriander leaves*
- *1 teaspoon ground cummin*
- *2 ripe tomatoes, diced*
- *sprig of fresh coriander*

Beat eggs until well mixed. Add milk, salt and pepper. Heat oil in a large, heavy frying pan and fry spring onions, chillies and ginger over low heat, stirring frequently, until soft. Add chopped coriander leaves and ground cummin, then egg mixture. Cook over low heat, stirring and folding egg as it begins to set. Cook only until eggs are of a creamy consistency—they will continue to cook with their stored heat. Turn onto a serving plate and garnish with tomato and coriander. Particularly good with chapatis or other flat breads.

CHICKEN WITH BEAN THREAD NOODLES

- *1 x 1.8 kg (3½ lb) chicken*
- *6 large dried shiitake (Chinese) mushrooms*
- *250 g (8 oz) bean thread vermicelli*
- *1 tablespoon oil*
- *1 large onion, sliced*
- *4 cloves garlic, crushed*
- *1 tablespoon fish sauce*
- *½ teaspoon paprika*
- *¼ teaspoon turmeric*
- *12 spring onions, finely sliced*
- *pepper and salt*

Remove any fat from cavity of chicken. Place whole chicken in a large saucepan, cover with water and bring to boil. Simmer over low heat, covered, until chicken is almost tender. Meanwhile soak shiitake mushrooms in hot water to cover for 30 minutes. Squeeze out excess water, discard stems and chop mushroom caps. Soak bean thread vermicelli in water to soften, then cut into 5 cm (2 inch) lengths.

Lift chicken out and set aside to cool a little. Strain stock and chill. Remove bones and skin from chicken and cut meat into large pieces. Heat oil in a large pan and fry onion and garlic over low heat, stirring, until soft and golden.

Skim any fat from surface of reserved chicken stock. Pour 2 tablespoons hot water over paprika and turmeric and add to pan with chicken stock. Bring to boil; add noodles and chopped mushrooms, then simmer for 15 minutes. Add chicken pieces and fish sauce and simmer for a few minutes. Add spring onions, pepper and salt to taste.

LEMON CHICKEN SALAD

- *750 g (1½ lb) chicken breast fillets*
  - *few celery leaves*
  - *1 large onion, halved*
- *3 tablespoons Chinese bottled lemon sauce*
  - *1½ tablespoons dark soy sauce*
- *⅓ cup finely chopped fresh coriander leaves and stems*
  - *1½ teaspoons finely grated fresh ginger*
  - *half a Chinese cabbage*

Cook chicken breast pieces with celery leaves and onion as described in recipe for Honey and Sesame Chicken (see p. 42). Cool and slice as described.

Combine lemon sauce and soy sauce in a small bowl. Pour over chicken and leave to marinate for at least 30 minutes. Arrange on a serving dish and serve sprinkled with a mixture of chopped coriander and grated ginger on a bed of shredded Chinese cabbage.

A Japanese dish so named for the domburi (the lidded earthenware bowl in which it is served).

CHICKEN AND EGG DOMBURI

- *500 g (1 lb) short grain rice*
- *1 whole chicken breast fillet or 2 thigh fillets*
- *2 cups Chicken Stock (see p. 10)*
- *¼ cup mirin or dry sherry*
- *¼ cup Japanese soy sauce (low salt, if preferred)*
- *6 eggs*
- *6 spring onions, thinly sliced*

Wash rice in cold water and drain for 30 minutes. Place in a heavy based saucepan with a well-fitting lid. Add 3 cups cold water and bring quickly to boil. Cover pan, turn heat low and cook for 15 minutes without lifting lid. Return heat to high for 20 seconds then remove pan from heat (do not lift lid) and allow to stand for 10 minutes before serving.

Meanwhile cut chicken into small dice. Pour stock into a saucepan and bring to boil with mirin and soy sauce. Add diced chicken; return to boil. Cover, reduce heat and simmer just until colour changes.

Gently stir eggs only until yolks break, adding salt if desired. Add eggs with ¾ of the spring onions to simmering stock. Let mixture return to boil—do not stir—then turn heat very low. Cover and cook for about 3 minutes until eggs are set but still soft.

Transfer rice to heated serving bowl. Ladle hot chicken and egg mixture over. Garnish with remaining spring onions and serve immediately.

CHICKEN WITH RICE AND MUSHROOMS

- *500 g (1 lb) short grain rice*
- *8 dried shiitake (Chinese) mushrooms*
- *1/3 cup Japanese soy sauce*
- *1/3 cup mirin or dry sherry*
- *4 teaspoons sugar*
- *375 g (12 oz) chicken breast fillets, thinly sliced*
- *oil for frying*
- *1 cup cooked green peas*

Wash rice thoroughly and leave it to drain in a sieve for 30 minutes. Place rice in a saucepan with 3 cups water and bring to boil. Turn heat very low, cover pan and cook for 20 minutes without lifting lid.

Pour boiling water to cover mushrooms, soak for 30 minutes. Remove mushrooms from water, reserving water. Discard stems. Place caps in a small saucepan with 1/2 cup of soaking water and half of each quantity of soy, mirin and sugar. Cover and simmer until very little liquid is left. Remove mushrooms and set aside to cool.

Pour about 1/4 cup remaining mushroom water into the same pan; add remaining soy, mirin and sugar. Stir to dissolve sugar. Add sliced chicken; bring to boil, then turn heat low. Cover and simmer gently for 3 minutes. Turn off heat and leave covered.

Turn cooked rice into a large earthenware bowl with lid. Spread chicken on top and spoon liquid from chicken over surface. Slice mushrooms and sprinkle over chicken. Garnish with green peas. Serve hot.

HONEY AND SESAME CHICKEN

- *750 g (1½ lb) chicken fillets*
- *few celery leaves*
- *1 large onion, halved*
- *1 teaspoon honey*
- *1 tablespoon oyster sauce*
- *2 tablespoons light soy sauce*
- *salt to taste*
- *¼ teaspoon five spice powder*
- *½ cup finely chopped spring onions*
- *1 tablespoon finely grated fresh ginger*
- *1 tablespoon toasted sesame seeds*

Place chicken fillets in a saucepan with water to cover. Add celery leaves and onion and slowly bring just to simmering point. Cover and poach over very gentle heat for 6 to 8 minutes. Turn off heat and allow chicken to cool in liquid. (Strain liquid, chill, then skim off fat. Reserve this stock for a future use.) Slice meat thinly. Arrange on a platter.

Mix honey, oyster sauce, soy sauce, salt and spice powder in a small bowl until well blended. Spoon over chicken. Cover and leave for 30 minutes. Before serving, mix spring onions and ginger and sprinkle over chicken. Top with sesame seeds.

TANGERINE CHICKEN

- 1 x 1.8 kg (3½ lb) roasting chicken
- 1½ tablespoons light soy sauce
- salt to taste
- 1 teaspoon sugar
- 1½ tablespoons dry sherry
- 1 piece dried tangerine peel, about the size of a bay leaf
- 1 whole star anise
- 3 tablespoons brown sugar (see Note)
- fresh coriander sprigs to garnish

Remove fat from chicken cavity. Wash chicken and dry with paper towels. Mix soy sauce, salt, sugar and dry sherry in a wide dish. Rub mixture inside and outside chicken. Marinate for 20 minutes, turning chicken twice. Place in a steamer and steam for 25 minutes.

Crush tangerine peel and star anise with a mortar and pestle as finely as possible and mix with brown sugar. Take a large, heavy saucepan or flameproof casserole with a well-fitting lid, deep enough to hold whole chicken on a rack or trivet. Line base with heavy duty foil, bringing it a little way up the side of pan. Sprinkle tangerine mixture evenly over foil, then place a trivet or wire rack on top. Place chicken on rack. Cover pan tightly and put over medium heat. When smoke begins to escape under lid, turn heat very low and smoke chicken for 20 minutes, or until done.

You can serve this dish hot or at room temperature. Slice flesh off bones and arrange on a platter. Garnish with sprigs of coriander.

Note The brown sugar is used for the smoking process only and does not add kilojoules to the dish.

Chicken with Vegetables in Oyster Sauce

- 750 g (1½ lbs) chicken breast meat, skin removed
- salt and pepper to taste
- 1 tablespoon cornflour
- 2 egg whites
- 2 cups sliced cauliflower
- 1½ tablespoons peanut oil
- 1 teaspoon finely grated fresh ginger
- 1 large clove garlic, crushed
- 8 spring onions, cut in bite-size pieces
- 1 red and 1 green capsicum, finely sliced
- 3 tablespoons oyster sauce

Cut chicken into bite-size pieces and place in a bowl. Season with salt and pepper, then sprinkle with cornflour and 2 teaspoons peanut oil, mix and set aside for 15 minutes. Add unbeaten egg whites; mix well and chill for 30 minutes.

Bring a large saucepan of lightly salted water to boil. Add chicken pieces in small batches and cook for 2 minutes. Lift chicken out with a wire strainer and drain in a colander.

Drop slices of cauliflower into lightly salted boiling water and boil for 1 minute. Drain in colander and refresh in a bowl of iced water. Heat remaining oil in a wok and add ginger, garlic, spring onions and capsicums. Stir-fry on high heat for 1 minute. Add oyster sauce mixed with 2 tablespoons water. Stir in cauliflower and chicken pieces until heated through. Serve with rice.

BRAISED CHICKEN WITH MUSHROOMS

- *12 small chicken thighs, skin removed and fat trimmed*
  - *3 tablespoons dry sherry*
  - *3 tablespoons light soy sauce*
  - *2 large cloves garlic, crushed*
  - *2 teaspoons finely grated fresh ginger*
  - *1 teaspoon five spice powder*
- *12 dried shiitake (Chinese) mushrooms*
  - *1 tablespoon peanut oil*
  - *250 g (8 oz) snow peas*
  - *1 teaspoon cornflour*

If you can only get large chicken thighs, halve the number. Mix sherry, soy sauce, garlic, ginger and five spice powder in a large bowl and marinate chicken pieces for 30 minutes. Soak mushrooms in hot water for 30 minutes. Discard stems.

Drain chicken pieces, reserving marinade. Heat a wok and add oil, swirling to coat surface. Stir-fry chicken over medium heat until pieces change colour. Toss so that all surfaces come in contact with heat. Stir in reserved marinade, 1 cup of mushroom water and mushrooms. Bring to boil, then lower heat. Cover and simmer for 20 to 25 minutes.

String snow peas and blanch in boiling salted water for 1 minute. Refresh in iced water. Mix cornflour with 1 tablespoon of cold water. Stir into cooked chicken, allow to boil and thicken. Serve immediately garnished with snow peas.

Salads

Beef Salad

- 500 g (1 lb) rump, fillet or sirloin steak
- 1 teaspoon chopped garlic
- 1 tablespoon chopped coriander roots and stalks
- 1 teaspoon green peppercorns in brine, drained
- 2 teaspoons raw sugar or palm sugar
- 2 teaspoons Maggi Seasoning
- 1 tablespoon lime juice
- 2 teaspoons fish sauce
- 2 small seedless cucumbers
- 8 small purple shallots or 2 small purple onions, sliced thinly
- 3 red chillies, seeded and sliced
- 1 stem lemon grass (tender white part only) sliced thinly
- fresh mint sprigs

Trim fat from steak. Barbecue over coals for best flavour, otherwise grill under preheated griller until medium rare. Cool until firm, then cut into thin slices.

Pound or crush garlic with coriander, peppercorns and sugar. Add Maggi Seasoning, lime juice and fish sauce; stir until smooth. Peel cucumber, score with a fork and slice finely.

Lightly toss all ingredients except mint. Serve in a salad bowl garnished with fresh mint.

Chicken and Cucumber Salad

- *375 g (12 oz) chicken breast fillets*
  - *3 teaspoons fish sauce*
  - *3 tablespoons lime juice*
    - *2 teaspoons sugar*
- *3 small green seedless cucumbers, finely sliced*
  - *3 red chillies, seeded and finely sliced*
    - *lettuce leaves*
    - *fresh mint*

Steam chicken breast. Slice when cool.

Combine fish sauce, lime juice and sugar, stirring to dissolve sugar. Mix gently with chicken, cucumbers and chillies. Serve on lettuce leaves, garnished with mint.

Mango Salad

- *3 unripe mangoes, or green apples,*
  peeled and cut into julienne strips
- *salt to taste*
- *2 tablespoons lime juice*
- *1 tablespoon peanut oil*
- *3 teaspoons dried garlic flakes*
- *6 spring onions, thinly sliced*
- *185 g (6 oz) lean pork fillet, finely chopped*
- *1½ tablespoons dried shrimp, reduced to floss in electric blender*
- *1½ tablespoons fish sauce*
- *1 teaspoon palm sugar or brown sugar*
- *1 tablespoon crushed roasted peanuts*
- *2 red chillies, seeded and finely sliced*

Place fruit in a serving bowl. Sprinkle with salt and 1 tablespoon lime juice; mix gently. Heat oil in a wok and fry garlic flakes on gentle heat until pale golden—watch that they don't burn. Lift out with a slotted spoon and drain on paper towel. In the same oil quickly fry spring onions, just until soft. Remove and set aside. Add pork to wok and stir-fry quickly, tossing until evenly browned. Mix in shrimp floss, fish sauce, remaining tablespoon lime juice and palm sugar. Remove from heat. When ready to serve add pork mixture to fruit in bowl and toss lightly. Serve garnished with peanuts and chillies.

You will find green pawpaws in stores selling fresh Asian ingredients. For this dish, the pawpaws are not just under-ripe: they are so immature that the flesh is quite white and the seeds barely formed.

GREEN PAWPAW SALAD

- 3 tablespoons dried shrimp
- 1½ tablespoons crushed roasted peanuts
- 2 cloves garlic
- 3 purple shallots, or 1 medium purple onion
- 2 fresh red chillies, seeded
- 3 teaspoons fish sauce
- 3 teaspoons palm sugar or raw sugar
- 1 green pawpaw, peeled and finely shredded or grated
- 1 cup snake beans or tender green beans, cut into pieces
- ¼ cup lime juice, or to taste

Put dried shrimp in a food processor or blender and pulverise. Mix with peanuts and set aside. Roughly chop garlic, purple shallots and chillies. Pound together in a mortar and pestle with fish sauce and sugar. Add pawpaw shreds and beans and pound lightly to bruise and combine with other ingredients. Turn into a large bowl, add lime juice and mix. Taste and add more lime juice or fish sauce if necessary. Pile onto a serving platter and sprinkle with shrimp and peanut mixture.

A Thai salad traditionally made with pomelo, which resembles a giant grapefruit. However, as pomelo are difficult to find outside South East Asia, grapefruit may be substituted.

GRAPEFRUIT SALAD

- *4 grapefruit, pink and white varieties if possible*
- *2 small cloves garlic, roughly chopped*
- *2 red chillies, seeded and sliced*
- *1 tablespoon raw sugar or palm sugar*
- *2 tablespoons fish sauce*
- *1/3 cup lime juice*
- *1/2 cup dried shrimp, pulverised in electric blender*
- *2 stems lemon grass, sliced very finely*

Peel fruit with a sharp knife, removing rind and pith to expose flesh. Segment by cutting between membranes. Discard seeds and place segments in a bowl.

Pound garlic and one chilli in a mortar with raw sugar, fish sauce and lime juice. Mix with shrimp floss and lemon grass and sprinkle over grapefruit segments. Add remaining sliced chilli. Mix gently and serve at room temperature.

CARROT AND RADISH SALAD

- *1½ cups carrots, shredded or cut into short julienne strips*
- *2 cups white radish (daikon), shredded or cut into short julienne strips*
- *½ cup sliced spring onions, including some green tops*
- *salt to taste*
- *1 tablespoon caster sugar*
- *⅓ cup rice vinegar or white wine vinegar*
- *1 teaspoon wasabi (green horseradish) powder*

Put carrots, radish and spring onions in a bowl. Sprinkle salt over and rub into ingredients. Cover with cold water and let stand for 20 to 30 minutes. Drain and rinse again with cold water. Drain, squeezing out as much water as possible. Add sugar and rub in well. Sprinkle with vinegar and wasabi mixed with 1 tablespoon water. Mix well. (If wasabi is unavailable substitute hot English mustard.) Transfer to a serving bowl.

Substitute 500 g green beans when asparagus is hard to get.

ASPARAGUS SALAD

- 2 bunches fresh green asparagus
- 1½ cups strained, cold Chinese Chicken Stock (see p. 10)
- 2 tablespoons sesame seeds
- 1 teaspoon sugar
- 1½ tablespoons light soy sauce
- 3 teaspoons white wine vinegar
- 1½ tablespoons water

If using beans, top, tail and cut diagonally into even lengths. Snap tough ends off asparagus and discard. Cut into long diagonal slices. Blanch vegetables in boiling water 1 to 2 minutes, until tender but still crisp. Drain, place in bowl and cover immediately with stock. Leave to cool in stock.

Toast sesame seeds in dry pan over moderate heat, stirring until all are evenly golden brown. Cool on a plate. Crush in blender or mortar and pestle. Mix in remaining ingredients. Drain vegetables well and just before serving pour dressing over.

Serve as an accompaniment to a rice and curry meal or with Indian flat breads.

ONION AND CORIANDER SALAD

- *3 medium onions, thinly sliced*
- *salt to taste*
- *¼ cup lemon juice*
- *½ cup fresh coriander leaves, roughly chopped*

Combine all ingredients in a bowl. Cover and chill until serving time.

CABBAGE SALAD

- *1 large onion, finely sliced*
- *2 teaspoons salt*
- *¼ cup dried shrimp*
- *4 cups finely shredded red and green cabbage*
- *2 teaspoons palm sugar or brown sugar*
- *3 tablespoons lime juice*
- *¼ teaspoon ground black pepper*
- *1 clove garlic, crushed*
- *1 teaspoon pounded fresh coriander roots and stems*
- *3 teaspoons fish sauce*
- *coriander sprigs*

In a bowl, sprinkle onions with salt and leave for 20 minutes. Soak dried shrimp in hot water to cover for 10 minutes, then remove any sandy streaks.

Drain shrimp and pound lightly. Place in a bowl with red and green cabbage. Rinse salted onions in cold water, drain well. Stir palm sugar, lime juice, pepper, garlic, coriander and fish sauce until sugar dissolves. Combine with onions and cabbage and mix well. Serve garnished with coriander sprigs.

BEAN THREAD SALAD WITH WATER CHESTNUTS

- *100 g (3½ oz) broad bean thread noodles*
- *4 dried chillies*
- *½ cup dried shrimp*
- *1 teaspoon crushed garlic*
- *1 stem lemon grass (tender white part only), finely sliced*
- *2 tablespoons fish sauce*
- *3 tablespoons lime juice*
- *3 teaspoons raw sugar or palm sugar*
- *1 x 185 g (6 oz) can water chestnuts, sliced*
- *½ cup finely sliced spring onions*
- *basil and coriander sprigs*

Cook bean thread noodles in boiling water for 10 minutes, drain in a colander and cut into short lengths.

Cut tops off chillies and shake out seeds. Cut chillies into large pieces with scissors. Soak in warm water with dried shrimp for 10 minutes to soften.

Place chillies, shrimp, garlic and half the lemon grass in a blender with a little soaking water. Blend until smooth. Add fish sauce, lime juice and sugar and set aside.

Mix noodles with water chestnuts, spring onions and remaining lemon grass. Add blended chilli mixture and toss thoroughly. Garnish with basil and coriander leaves. Serve.

A sour and salty, slightly hot dressing accentuates some very different flavours in the fruit. Vary the fruit according to what is in season.

THAI CHICKEN, PRAWN AND FRUIT SALAD

- *1 mango, peeled and sliced*
- *1 orange, peeled and segmented*
- *1 pink or white grapefruit, peeled and segmented*
- *washed and dried lettuce leaves*
- *half a ripe pineapple*
- *1 x 185 g (6 oz) can water chestnuts, sliced finely*
- *6 miniature tomatoes, washed and chilled*
- *1 cup small seedless grapes, washed and chilled*
- *2 chicken breast fillets, poached and sliced*
- *375 g (12 oz) cooked prawns, shelled and deveined*
- *2 tablespoons roasted salted peanuts, crushed*

Arrange mango, orange and grapefruit on lettuce leaves. Peel pineapple with a sharp stainless steel knife. Quarter lengthwise, discard core, then cut in thin slices. Arrange on platter. Combine water chestnuts, tomatoes and grapes with chicken and prawns in a bowl. Sprinkle 2 tablespoons of Dressing over, tossing to distribute flavours. Mound chicken and prawn mixture on platter beside arranged fruits. Place remaining Dressing in a small serving bowl on platter with fruit for spooning over individual servings. Sprinkle crushed peanuts over salad just before serving.

DRESSING
- *1 tablespoon sugar*
- *2 tablespoons fish sauce*
- *2 tablespoons lime juice*
- *2 red chillies, seeded and sliced*
- *2 small cloves garlic, crushed to a smooth paste with 1 teaspoon of the sugar*

Dissolve sugar in ¼ cup cold water, then stir in remaining ingredients.

To prevent seafood becoming tough and rubbery, it is imperative to avoid overcooking.

SEAFOOD SALAD

- 375 g (12 oz) raw prawns
- 375 g (12 oz) cleaned squid
- 3 kaffir lime leaves, fresh or dried
- 3 sprigs fresh coriander
- 1 stalk lemon grass, finely sliced
- 1 tablespoon fish sauce
- 3 tablespoons lime juice
- 1 teaspoon dark brown sugar
- 2 cloves garlic, crushed
- 2 teaspoons finely chopped ginger
- freshly ground black pepper
- ¾ cup finely sliced spring onions, including some green tops
- ⅓ cup lightly packed mint leaves
- 2 or 3 fresh red chillies, finely sliced

Shell and devein prawns, (leaving tails on if desired). Slit and rinse squid tubes. Wipe clean with kitchen paper if needed. With a sharp knife, score inside surface diagonally with narrow parallel lines, holding the knife at an angle of 45 degrees to make cuts without going through. Cut scored squid into bite-size pieces.

Boil 3 cups of water in a small saucepan with lime leaves,

coriander and lemon grass for 5 minutes. Drop in squid and immediately the pieces curl and turn opaque, remove with a slotted spoon. This should take less than 1 minute. Bring liquid back to boil and cook prawns, only until they turn pink. Lift out immediately with slotted spoon.

In a serving bowl mix fish sauce, lime juice, sugar, garlic, ginger and pepper. Toss seafood in dressing, then add spring onions, mint and chillies and toss lightly.

Grilled eggplant adds a distinctive, smoky flavour to this dish.

Grilled Eggplant and Dried Shrimp

- *6 long, slender eggplants*
- *1 large clove garlic, finely chopped*
- *2 teaspoons sugar*
- *salt to taste*
- *2 tablespoons lime juice*
- *1½ tablespoons fish sauce*
- *⅓ cup dried shrimp*
- *1 red chilli, finely chopped*
- *fresh coriander or mint sprigs*

Wash and dry eggplants. Slice in halves lengthwise, place on foil-lined tray and char under a hot griller. When cool enough to handle, carefully peel off charred skin. Arrange on a dish.

Crush garlic with sugar and salt. Add to lime juice and fish sauce; stir until sugar dissolves. Spoon dressing evenly over eggplants.

Pulverise dried shrimp in food processor or blender. Sprinkle over eggplants. Garnish with chilli and coriander or mint. Serve at room temperature.

Almost every Thai meal includes raw vegetables eaten with a dipping sauce, as much for the health benefits as the pleasure of eating. Nam Prik is Thai for a variety of sauces both cooked and uncooked, based on fish sauce, dried shrimp and chilli. The best way to make nam prik is with a mortar and pestle. You can use an electric blender but the consistency will be different; it becomes too liquid. The sauce should have enough 'body' to coat the vegetables. Serve this dish as an appetiser.

VEGETABLES WITH NAM PRIK

- ½ cup small dried shrimp (see Note)
- 2 cloves garlic, chopped
- 4 shallots or 2 small red onions, chopped
- 3 fresh red chillies, chopped
- 2 limes
- 3 teaspoons palm sugar or brown sugar
- 4 tablespoons fish sauce

Rinse dried shrimp and soak in hot water for 10 minutes. Remove any sandy veins.

In a mortar, pound drained shrimp with garlic, shallots and chillies, until reduced to a paste. Juice limes on citrus juicer and discard seeds but add pulp and juice gradually to pounded mixture. Stir in palm sugar, fish sauce and 2 tablespoons cold water. Serve in a bowl surrounded with seasonal vegetables, raw or lightly blanched. If blanching, cook until barely tender, then plunge into iced water to stop cooking and fix colour.

SUGGESTED VEBETABLES Asparagus, stringless beans, tender carrots, spring onions, radishes, seedless cucumbers, cabbage. Cut into convenient sizes for dipping and arrange attractively.

Note Select dried shrimp which are salmon pink and yield to finger pressure through the packet. Those which are very hard and woody and faded in colour are probably older and while not bad, will be harder to pound.

VEGETABLES

Nothing could be simpler—on its own with rice, or as an extra vegetable accompaniment to a Chinese meal.

CRISP GREENS IN OYSTER SAUCE

- *500 g (1 lb) fresh green asparagus or tender stringless green beans or Chinese mustard cabbage or broccoli*
  - *2 tablespoons oyster sauce*
    - *2 teaspoons sugar*

Wash asparagus and snap off ends if tough. Bring to boil 6 cups water and drop in asparagus. When water returns to boil, cook for 2 minutes (for very slender spears), or until tender but still crunchy. (This will depend on thickness of asparagus.) Remove asparagus with slotted spoon and arrange on a warm serving dish. Heat ¼ cup cold water with oyster sauce and sugar, stirring. Bring to boil, spoon over vegetables and serve immediately.

If using beans, wash, trim and cut in halves. Cook in boiling water as for asparagus, but allow enough time for beans to be tender. Drain. Continue as above.

If using broccoli, divide into florets, keeping some stem on each. Cooking time will be less than 2 minutes.

If using Chinese mustard cabbage, wash well, cut stems into bite-size lengths, discarding ends of leaves. Cook 3 minutes.

Spicy Beans, Indian Style

- *750 g (1½ lb) green beans*
- *1 tablespoon oil*
- *1 teaspoon black mustard seeds*
- *sprig fresh curry leaves or 10 dried curry leaves*
- *1 large onion, finely chopped*
- *1 teaspoon finely grated fresh ginger*
- *1 teaspoon ground turmeric*
- *½ teaspoon cummin seeds*
- *½ teaspoon chilli powder, optional*
- *salt to taste*
- *4 ripe tomatoes, chopped*

Top, tail and string beans. Cut in short lengths. Heat oil and fry mustard seeds and curry leaves until seeds start to pop. Add onion and ginger, cook over low heat, stirring frequently, until onion is golden. Add turmeric, cummin seeds, chilli powder and salt and fry, stirring, for 2 minutes. Add tomatoes and cook, stirring, until reduced to a pulp. Stir in beans. Cover pan and cook just until beans are tender. Transfer to a serving dish.

Pulses are an important source of protein in India. Prepared this way they are both nourishing and tasty. Serve with rice or Indian flat breads.

INDIAN-STYLE BLACK-EYED BEANS

- 1½ cups black-eyed beans
- 3 cardamom pods, bruised
- 1 tablespoon chopped garlic
- 1 teaspoon turmeric
- salt to taste
- 3 large onions, roughly chopped
- 1 tablespoon chopped fresh ginger
- 2 dried red chillies, seeded
- 1 tablespoon oil
- 1½ teaspoons ground cummin
- ¾ cup low-fat plain yoghurt
- 1 teaspoon garam masala
- ¼ cup chopped fresh coriander leaves

Wash beans thoroughly, cover in cold water and soak overnight. Drain beans, put in a saucepan with fresh cold water to cover and bring to boil with cardamom pods, 1 teaspoon of garlic and turmeric. Cover and simmer 30 minutes. Add salt and cook until tender. Drain, reserving liquid.

Purée remaining garlic, onions, ginger and chillies in a blender or food processor. Heat oil and cook blended mixture over low heat, stirring. When it starts to brown, add cummin and fry for a few more seconds. Mix yoghurt with ¾ cup of reserved cooking liquid until well blended. Add yoghurt mixture and drained beans and cook 5 minutes longer or until gravy is reduced and thick. Sprinkle with garam masala and coriander leaves.

After trying this recipe, you'll never throw away another broccoli stem.

BROCCOLI, CHINESE STYLE

- *1 large bunch broccoli*
- *salt*
- *1 tablespoon peanut oil*
- *1 teaspoon grated fresh ginger*
- *1 tablespoon oyster sauce*
- *1 tablespoon light soy sauce*
- *1 teaspoon sugar*
- *½ teaspoon sesame oil*
- *2 teaspoons cornflour*

Cut flowerheads from broccoli stems, divide into florets and set aside. Peel stems and slice into bite-size pieces, cutting thick stems in half lengthwise. Boil a small amount of lightly salted water in a saucepan and drop in stems. When water returns to boil, cover and cook for 1 minute, then add florets. Cook 1 minute or until bright green and barely tender. Lift out with a slotted spoon. Reserve ½ cup of cooking water.

In a wok, heat peanut oil and stir-fry ginger for 30 seconds. Add oyster sauce, soy sauce, sugar, sesame oil and reserved cooking liquid and bring to boil. Blend cornflour with 1 tablespoon of cold water, add and stir until it boils and thickens. Toss in broccoli pieces to coat with sauce and serve hot.

CHICK PEAS IN SPICY TOMATO SAUCE

- *1½ cups dried chick peas*
- *1 or 2 bay leaves*
- *1 teaspoon ground turmeric*
- *salt to taste*
- *1 tablespoon oil*
- *3 large onions, finely chopped*
- *3 cloves garlic, chopped*
- *1 tablespoon finely chopped fresh ginger*
- *1½ teaspoons garam masala*
- *3 large ripe tomatoes, peeled and chopped*
- *1 fresh green chilli, seeded and sliced*
- *¼ cup chopped fresh mint leaves*
- *salt to taste*

Cover chick peas with cold water and soak overnight. Drain, rinse and place in a heavy saucepan with bay leaves and turmeric. Cover with water. Bring to boil, cover and simmer till almost tender. Add salt, cook until done. Drain, reserving liquid.

In a heavy based pan heat oil and fry onion, garlic and ginger over low heat, stirring frequently, until golden. Add garam masala, tomatoes, chilli, drained chick peas and half the mint; stir well to mix. Add ½ cup reserved cooking liquid, cover and simmer, stirring occasionally, until peas are tender and tomatoes reduced to a purée. Add salt and sprinkle with remaining mint.

Braised Chinese Cabbage

- *750g (1½ lb) Chinese cabbage (wongah bak) and Chinese mustard cabbage (gai choy)*
- *1 tablespoon peanut oil*
- *1 teaspoon crushed garlic*
- *1 teaspoon finely grated fresh ginger*
- *¾ cup Chinese Chicken Stock (see p. 10)*
- *1½ tablespoons light soy sauce*
- *2 teaspoons cornflour*
- *½ teaspoon sesame oil*

Remove any tough leaf tips, leaving a narrow border on mid rib. Cut through into bite-size pieces. In a wok heat oil and stir-fry garlic and ginger a few seconds, add cabbage and stir-fry for 1 minute. Add stock and soy sauce. Cook, covered, for 2 minutes, or until cabbage is tender but still crunchy. Mix cornflour with 1 tablespoon cold water and stir into sauce. Cook, stirring, until it boils and thickens. Add sesame oil, toss to mix and serve.

Spicy Cauliflower

- 1 small cauliflower, or half large cauliflower
- 1 tablespoon oil
- 2 teaspoons panch phora
- 3 cloves garlic, chopped
- 2 teaspoons finely grated fresh ginger
- 1 teaspoon ground turmeric
- salt to taste

Separate cauliflower into florets and cut in slices, making sure some of stalk is attached to each piece. Heat oil in a large pan, add panch phora and fry for 1 minute or until mustard seeds start to pop. Add garlic and ginger and saute until garlic is golden. Stir in turmeric. Add cauliflower slices and fry, stirring constantly, over low heat for a few minutes. Add salt and about ¼ cup water, cover and steam for a further 3 to 4 minutes until cauliflower is just tender—it should not be overcooked. Serve with rice.

Especially good in winter when a chilled salad doesn't seem tempting.

STIR-FRIED LETTUCE

- *1 large, firm iceberg lettuce*
- *1 tablespoon peanut oil*
- *1 teaspoon crushed garlic*
- *1 teaspoon finely grated fresh ginger*
- *salt to taste*
- *1 teaspoon sugar*
- *1 tablespoon light soy sauce*

Wash lettuce, drain and dry well. Cut in half lengthwise, then make 2 or 3 cuts lengthwise and the same across to give chunky, bite-size pieces.

Heat a wok, add peanut oil, garlic and ginger and stir-fry for 10 seconds, then add lettuce and stir-fry for a further 30 to 40 seconds. Remove from heat, add salt, sugar and soy sauce. Toss and serve immediately.

YOGHURT WITH SPINACH

- *1 large bunch spinach*
- *2 teaspoons oil*
- *2 teaspoons panch phora*
- *1 teaspoon ground coriander*
- *½ teaspoon chilli powder*
- *salt to taste*
- *2 cups low-fat plain yoghurt*

Wash spinach thoroughly, remove tough stems and put wet leaves into a saucepan. Cover and steam over low heat until spinach is tender. Cool, squeeze and chop finely.

In a small pan heat oil and fry panch phora until mustard seeds start to pop. Add coriander and continue to fry, stirring, for 2 minutes. Remove from heat, stir in chilli powder and salt and leave to cool. Mix in yoghurt and spinach. Serve at room temperature as a side dish with rice and curry or chapatis.

BRAISED BEAN CURD AND VEGETABLES

- 1 tablespoon peanut oil
- 1 large clove garlic, crushed
- 500 g (1 lb) mixed vegetables of choice, cut into bite-size pieces—baby corn, snow peas, button mushrooms, gai lara
- ½ cup chicken or vegetable stock
- 2 tablespoons oyster sauce
- 1 tablespoon soy sauce
- 1½ tablespoons sherry
- 2 teaspoons cornflour
- 500 g (1 lb) fresh bean curd sliced

Heat oil in a wok, swirling to coat surface. Add garlic and fry for 10 seconds. Add vegetables and stir-fry for 2 minutes. Add stock, cover and simmer for 1 minute longer. Mix oyster sauce, soy sauce and sherry. Add to wok, stir and simmer. Mix cornflour with 1 tablespoon cold water. Add to wok, stirring until it boils and thickens. Add bean curd; heat through and serve immediately.

In India fresh cheese or panir is made at home with full cream milk. Apart from the time and labour saved, it is better to use ricotta because, being made from whey, it is very low in fat.

PEAS AND FRESH CHEESE CURRY

- 375 g (12 oz) fresh baked ricotta cheese (see Note)
- 1 tablespoon oil
- 2 medium onions, finely chopped
- 3 cloves garlic, finely chopped
- 2 teaspoons finely grated ginger
- 2 teaspoons ground coriander
- 1 teaspoon ground cummin
- 1 teaspoon ground turmeric
- ½ teaspoon chilli powder
- 2 firm ripe tomatoes, peeled, seeded and chopped
- 250 g (8 oz) shelled fresh peas
- salt to taste
- 1 teaspoon garam masala
- 2 tablespoons finely chopped fresh coriander leaves

Cut baked ricotta into 2.5 cm (1 inch) cubes. Heat oil in a heavy pan and fry onions, garlic and ginger over low heat, stirring frequently, until golden. Add coriander, cummin, turmeric and chilli powder and stir for 1 minute longer. Then stir in tomatoes, peas and salt. Cook, covered, until tomatoes form a pulp and peas are almost done. Stir from time to time, adding a little hot water if mixture seems too dry.

Add cheese cubes and half of coriander. Simmer, covered, for 10 minutes more. Sprinkle with garam masala and remaining coriander. Serve hot with rice or flat bread.

Note It is possible to buy baked ricotta from Italian delicatessens, but it is simple (and cheaper) to make yourself. Purchase a 375 g (12 oz) block fresh ricotta. Wrap in a clean linen tea towel and leave for 1 hour so that excess moisture can be absorbed. Cut block in half and place on a non-stick or foil-lined baking tray. Bake in a moderate oven 20 minutes. Turn over with a frying slice and bake for a further 20 minutes—cheese will look golden brown. Set aside to cool before use.

SPICY DICED VEGETABLES

- 2 tablespoons vegetable oil
- 2 teaspoons black mustard seeds
- 2 onions, finely chopped
- 1 teaspoon finely chopped garlic
- 1 teaspoon finely grated fresh ginger
- 2 teaspoons ground coriander
- 2 teaspoons ground cummin
- pinch of chilli powder, optional
- 2 ripe red tomatoes, peeled, seeded and diced
- 3 large carrots, peeled and diced
- 3 medium size potatoes, peeled and diced
- 250 g (8 oz) tender green beans, cut into bite-size pieces
- 1 teaspoon salt
- ½ teaspoon garam masala

Heat oil in a saucepan or wok and fry mustard seeds until they pop. Add onions, garlic and ginger and fry, stirring, until golden. Add coriander, cummin and chilli powder and fry for a few seconds, then vegetables and salt, tossing until coated with spices and oil. Add ⅓ cup water, cover and cook for 20 minutes or until vegetables are tender, stirring gently every 5 minutes and adding a little extra water if necessary. When done, sprinkle with garam masala and serve with rice or chapatis.

CURRIED PEA PODS

- 500 g (1 lb) sugar snap peas or snow peas
- 1 tablespoon oil
- 1 medium onion, finely chopped
- 1 teaspoon finely chopped fresh ginger
- 1 teaspoon ground turmeric
- salt to taste
- 1 teaspoon garam masala
- ½ teaspoon chilli powder
- 2 ripe tomatoes, diced
- 4 small potatoes, peeled and diced

Wash peas and remove strings. Heat oil in a large, heavy frying pan and fry onion and ginger over low heat until onion is soft and golden. Add turmeric, salt, garam masala and chilli powder, stir for a minute or so, then add tomatoes and potatoes.

Stir well, cover and cook over low heat until potatoes are almost tender, stirring occasionally. Add sugar snap peas and cook for a few minutes longer, until they are tender but still crisp.

This curry is quite dry: there should be sufficient liquid from tomatoes, but if curry starts to stick to base of pan, add a little water. Serve with rice or chapatis.

Mixed Vegetables with Coconut

- 6 cups mixed vegetables of choice, cut into julienne strips—
  carrots, beans, zucchini, pumpkin, capsicum, eggplant, etc.
  - 3 tablespoons desiccated coconut
  - 1 teaspoon cummin seeds
  - 1 teaspoon chopped garlic
  - 2 fresh green chillies, seeded
  - ¼ cup coconut milk
  - salt to taste
- 2 sprigs fresh curry leaves or 12 dried curry leaves

In a saucepan boil just enough lightly salted water to cook vegetables. Boil each vegetable separately, one kind at a time, until tender but still crisp. Remove each batch with a slotted spoon and reserve in a bowl. Re-use water for all vegetables, adding a little more as it boils away—keep quantity small. Reserve cooking liquid. Put desiccated coconut into pan with liquid and when lukewarm blend with cummin seeds, garlic and chillies on high speed until coconut is very finely ground. Add this mixture to saucepan with coconut milk, ¼ cup water, salt and curry leaves. Add vegetables, stirring gently to coat and simmer uncovered for 5 minutes. Serve hot.

MEAT

STEAK IN PLUM SAUCE

- *500 g (1 lb) fillet or other tender steak*
- *2 tablespoons light soy sauce*
- *1 tablespoon dry sherry*
- *1 teaspoon grated ginger*
- *1 clove garlic, crushed with ½ teaspoon salt*
- *6 spring onions*
- *1 tablespoon oil*
- *2 tablespoons plum sauce*
- *finely shredded lettuce*

Remove any fat from beef. Cut across into 6 slices. Flatten slices with blade of cleaver. Mix soy sauce, sherry, ginger and garlic. Place beef in a bowl and pour mixture over, turning slices so that they are well coated. Leave to marinate for at least 1 hour.

Slice spring onions into bite-size pieces. Heat a wok; add half the oil, swirling to coat surface, and when hot fry 3 slices of beef, pressing against wok to brown both sides. Remove and reserve. Add remaining oil and cook remaining beef. Add spring onions, return first 3 slices of meat and toss briefly.

Stir in plum sauce with 2 tablespoons of water and heat through. Serve on a bed of finely shredded lettuce.

Lamb Curry

- 1.5 kg (3 lb) lean, boneless lamb
- 1 tablespoon oil
- 2 large onions, chopped
- 4 cloves garlic, chopped
- 1 tablespoon finely chopped fresh ginger
- 2 tablespoons good quality curry powder
- salt to taste
- 2 tablespoons vinegar or lemon juice
- 3 large tomatoes, seeded and chopped
- 2 fresh chillies, seeded and sliced
- ¼ cup chopped fresh mint leaves
- 1 teaspoon garam masala

Trim off fat and cut meat into cubes. Heat oil in a heavy based saucepan and fry onions, garlic and ginger over low heat until soft and golden, stirring frequently. Add curry powder, salt and vinegar or lemon juice and stir. Add lamb and cook, stirring and turning constantly, until cubes are coated with spice. Add tomatoes, chillies, and mint.

Cover and simmer until meat is tender, about 1¼ hours. Tomatoes should provide enough liquid for meat to cook in, but if you find mixture is sticking to pan add a little hot water—about ½ cup. Add garam masala and extra mint if liked during the last 5 minutes of cooking.

A favourite in the Philippines but usually much richer because the beef is larded with pork fat. We keep the flavour, drop the fat.

BEEF POT ROAST

- 1.5 kg (3 lb) blade steak in one piece
- 3 large onions, quartered
- 3 large tomatoes, halved
- 1 bay leaf
- ½ cup vinegar
- 3 cloves garlic, chopped
- 1 tablespoon finely chopped fresh ginger
- 2 tablespoons light soy sauce
- 6 potatoes, peeled and halved
- freshly ground black pepper

Trim any fat from beef and discard. Put meat into a deep, heavy saucepan or flameproof casserole just slightly larger than the beef. Surround with onions, tomatoes, bay leaf, vinegar, garlic, ginger and soy sauce. Bring to boil, then reduce heat, cover pan and simmer until meat is almost tender. Add potatoes and plenty of freshly ground pepper and simmer until potatoes are cooked. Baste meat from time to time. When cooked, slice meat and arrange on serving platter, adding sauce and potatoes.

A low-fat adaptation of the Japanese sukiyaki. If you have an electric frying pan, you can cook the dish at the table. Guests then help themselves from the pan. You will need a very tender steak for this dish—aged rump steak would be a good substitute for fillet.

QUICK-COOKED BEEF AND VEGETABLES

- *1 kg (2 lb) fillet steak or tender rump, in one piece*
- *3 small leeks*
- *1 x 565 g (1¼ lb) can baby corn cobs*
- *250g (8 oz) button mushrooms or canned shiitake mushrooms*
- *3 white onions*
- *250 g (8 oz) fresh bean sprouts*
- *1 small Chinese cabbage*
- *60 g (2 oz) bean thread vermicelli*
- *6 squares bean curd (tofu)*
- *oil for greasing pan*
- *Japanese soy sauce*
- *sugar*
- *sake (Japanese rice wine)*
- *beef stock*

Freeze steak until just firm and cut in paper-thin slices. Cut leeks into diagonal slices and drain corn cobs. Wipe mushroom caps, trim stalks and cut into halves. Peel onions and cut in small wedges. Wash and drain bean sprouts and pinch off tails. Discard outer leaves and cut Chinese cabbage into bite-size pieces. Cook noodles in boiling water for 10 minutes, drain. Set out all ingredients on a large platter.

Heat a large heavy frying pan and rub over with a little oil. Add half of each vegetable to pan and fry on high heat until just tender. Push to one side and add slices of meat in one layer. When cooked on one side (this will only take a short time because meat is so thinly sliced) turn and cook other side. Sprinkle with soy sauce, sugar and sake to taste. Add a little stock to moisten meat and vegetables. Mix in half the noodles and tofu and heat through. Serve immediately in individual bowls with hot steamed rice.

Remaining ingredients are added to the pan and cooked after the first batch has been eaten.

STIR-FRIED CHILLI BEEF

- 500 g (1 lb) lean fillet or rump steak, in one piece
- 1 tablespoon peanut oil
- 1 teaspoon finely chopped garlic
- 1 teaspoon finely chopped fresh ginger
- ¾ cup thinly sliced spring onions
- 1 teaspoon chilli sauce
- 90 g (3 oz) snow peas
- ½ cup thinly sliced celery
- 2 teaspoons cornflour
- ½ teaspoon sesame oil

Freeze steak until firm and then cut into paper-thin slices. Heat wok; add peanut oil and swirl to coat. Add garlic, ginger and half the spring onions. Stir-fry for 1 minute on low heat. Add meat and stir-fry on high heat, tossing meat so that all surfaces brown. Add chilli sauce, snow peas and celery and stir-fry for 30 seconds. Mix cornflour with ½ cup water and add to wok. Bring to boil, stirring, then add sesame oil and remaining spring onions. Mix and serve immediately.

FRIED BEEF WITH BAMBOO SHOOTS AND MUSHROOMS

- *500 g (1 lb) rump steak*
- *1½ tablespoons Pepper and Coriander Paste (see p. 2)*
- *4 cloves garlic, finely chopped*
- *1 tablespoon oil*
- *¾ cup sliced bamboo shoots*
- *¾ cup drained straw mushrooms*
- *2 red chillies, chopped and seeded*
- *½ cup fresh basil leaves*
- *1 tablespoon fish sauce*
- *1 teaspoon palm sugar or brown sugar*
- *3 tender fresh kaffir lime or citrus leaves, finely shredded*

Trim off fat from steak and partially freeze meat, so that you can slice meat into thin strips. Marinate with half the Pepper and Coriander Paste for 1 hour. Fry garlic in oil in a large pan over low heat, stirring constantly, for 1 minute—do not let it brown. Add remaining paste and fry, stirring until fragrant. Add beef and stir-fry over medium heat, until colour changes.

Add bamboo shoots and mushrooms (these may be cut in halves lengthwise so they absorb more flavour). Continue cooking until liquid is reduced. Stir in chillies, basil leaves, fish sauce, palm sugar and lime leaves and heat through. Serve with steamed rice or cooked bean thread vermicelli.

STIR-FRIED BEEF AND CUCUMBERS

- *375 g (12 oz) lean rump or fillet steak*
- *1 teaspoon sesame oil*
- *1½ tablespoons light soy sauce*
- *½ teaspoon sugar*
- *¼ teaspoon cayenne pepper*
- *2 green cucumbers*
- *1 tablespoon oil*
- *1 tablespoon toasted, crushed sesame seeds*

Trim off any fat and freeze beef for a short time to make it firm enough to cut into paper-thin slices. Slices should be about 5 cm (2 inch) long and 12 mm (½ inch) wide. Put beef in a bowl and mix in sesame oil, soy sauce, sugar and cayenne. Make sure meat is well coated so that flavours penetrate.

Peel cucumbers, but leave a thin strip of green at intervals to give a decorative effect. Cut in halves lengthwise and scoop out seeds with a small spoon. Cut across into medium-thin slices.

Heat oil in a wok, swirling to coat surface. Add beef and stir-fry on high heat for 1 minute. Add cucumbers and toss for a further minute. Let mixture simmer until cucumber is half cooked. It should be tender but still crisp. Garnish with sesame seeds and serve immediately.

STIR-FRIED PORK WITH LOTUS ROOT

- *500 g (1 lb) pork fillet or other lean pork*
  - *1 tablespoon light soy sauce*
    - *2 teaspoons dry sherry*
  - *1 small clove garlic, crushed*
  - *1 teaspoon finely grated fresh ginger*
  - *1 canned lotus root, sliced thinly*
    - *¾ cup stock*
  - *1 tablespoon oyster sauce*
  - *1 tablespoon dry sherry*
  - *½ teaspoon sesame oil*
  - *1 tablespoon peanut oil*
  - *2 teaspoons cornflour*
    - *cucumber slices*

Trim fat from pork and freeze meat until it is firm enough to cut into paper-thin slices. In a large bowl mix soy sauce, sherry, garlic and ginger. Add pork slices and mix well.

Mix stock, oyster sauce, sherry and sesame oil in a separate bowl. Heat a wok; add peanut oil and swirl to coat surface. Add marinated pork and stir-fry on high heat, tossing meat constantly, until browned. Add sauce mixture; bring to boil. Cover and simmer 5 minutes. Blend cornflour with 1 tablespoon cold water. Add to wok and stir until sauce boils and thickens. Add lotus root and heat through. Arrange on a dish and garnish with sliced cucumber.

CHILLI PORK WITH BROCCOLI

- *500 g (1 lb) pork fillet or other lean pork*
- *375 g (12 oz) broccoli*
- *1 tablespoon canned, salted black beans*
- *1 tablespoon dark soy sauce*
- *2 teaspoons chilli bean sauce (glossary)*
- *1 teaspoon sugar*
- *1 teaspoon cornflour*
- *1 tablespoon peanut oil*
- *1 clove garlic, crushed*
- *finely sliced red chilli*

Remove fat from pork and chill in freezer until firm. Cut into paper-thin slices. Cut broccoli into bite-size pieces and blanch in boiling water for 1 minute. Drain and set aside. Rinse black beans under cold water, drain and chop. Combine soy sauce, chilli bean sauce, sugar and cornflour with 4 tablespoons cold water.

Heat a wok, add oil and swirl to coat surface. Add pork and stir-fry over high heat, tossing until browned. Remove pork and set aside. Add garlic and chopped black beans; stir-fry for a few seconds. Stir in sauce mixture and cook until it boils and thickens. Return pork to wok with broccoli and stir together until heated through. Serve immediately, garnished with chilli.

Rice, Noodles, Bread

Short or medium grain rice, cooked by the absorption method, can be used to accompany Korean, Vietnamese, Chinese and Japanese dishes. The resulting product will be pearly and clinging, easy to pick up with chopsticks. Whatever kind of rice you cook, it is important to use a heavy based saucepan.

STEAMED RICE

- *2½ cups (500 g) short or medium grain rice*
- *3 cups cold water*

If necessary, wash rice in cold water. Leave to drain in a sieve or colander for at least 30 minutes. Place rice in a heavy based saucepan with a well-fitting lid. Add 3 cups cold water and bring rapidly to boil. Cover pan, turn heat very low and cook for 15 minutes without lifting lid. Remove pan from heat and set aside, covered, for 10 minutes before serving.

Note   For Indian, Indonesian or Thai meals, opt for long grain rice which will give an aromatic, fluffy result more suited to the cuisine of those countries. Since long grain rice has greater absorbency, increase water to 3½ cups for 500 g (1 lb) rice.

If you prefer to use natural brown (unpolished) rice with its benefits of extra fibre and B vitamins, use the same proportions as for long grain rice, but be prepared for it to take almost twice as long to cook, 35 to 40 minutes until all the liquid is absorbed.

An aromatic Indian rice ideal for curries, lentils and spicy vegetable dishes.

SAVOURY RICE

- *2½ cups basmati or Dehra Dun rice*
- *3½ cups hot water*
- *1 teaspoon ghee*
- *1½ teaspoons salt*
- *1 small stick cinnamon*
- *½ teaspoon ground turmeric*
- *2 cardamom pods*

Wash rice well in cold water and drain in a sieve for 30 minutes. Bring water, ghee, salt, cinnamon stick, turmeric and cardamom pods to boil in a heavy saucepan with a well-fitting lid. Add rice, stir and bring quickly back to boil. Turn heat very low, cover pan tightly and cook without lifting lid for 20 to 25 minutes. Lift lid to allow steam to escape for a few minutes. Lightly fluff up rice with a fork, taking care not to mash grains, which should be firm, separate and perfectly cooked. Discard cinnamon and cardamom. Serve using a slotted metal spoon, so as not to crush the grains.

Discs of Indian unleavened bread which have a chewy texture and delicious flavour. They can accompany roasted and skewered dishes, dry vegetable preparations and lentil dishes. In India cooked chapatis are held for a moment or two over the fire which makes them puff up like balloons. You can do this over a gas flame, holding them with kitchen tongs. Alternatively you can cook them on a griddle over a barbecue and hold them over the glowing coals.

CHAPATIS
Makes 20 to 24

- 3 cups fine wholemeal flour or roti flour
- 1 teaspoon salt or to taste
- 1 cup lukewarm water

Place flour in a mixing bowl, reserving about ½ cup for rolling out chapatis. Mix salt through flour; then add water all at once and mix to a firm but not stiff dough. Knead dough for at least 10 minutes—the more it is kneaded the lighter the bread will be. (You can also mix dough in a food processor which reduces the kneading time.) Form dough into a ball, cover with clear plastic wrap and stand for at least 1 hour.

Shape dough into walnut-size balls. Roll out each one on a lightly floured board, using reserved flour, to a very thin circle. Once all chapatis are rolled, heat a griddle plate or heavy frying pan until very hot, then reduce heat to medium and cook chapatis, starting with those that were rolled first (resting time makes chapatis lighter). Place chapati on griddle and leave for about 1 minute.

Turn and cook the other side for 1 minute more, pressing lightly around edges with a folded tea towel. This encourages bubbles to form. As each one is cooked, cover with a warm, clean tea towel until all are ready.

Note For a lighter chapati, use equal quantities of fine wholemeal flour and plain white flour. For a softer chapati, rub a scant two teaspoons of ghee or butter into flour before adding water.

Serve these noodles with soups, stir-fried or braised dishes.

Egg Noodles

Egg noodles are made with wheat flour and usually sold in 500 g (1 lb) packets, each containing about 7 bundles. It is important to soak these noodles in warm water for about 10 minutes before cooking them since the strands separate and cook more evenly.

Drain noodles from soaking water, drop into boiling water and boil fine noodles for 2 to 3 minutes and wide noodles for 3 to 4 minutes. They should be tender but firm to the bite. Drain immediately in a large colander, then rinse with cold water to get rid of excess starch and to stop the cooking process. Drain thoroughly. You can reheat noodles in the colander by pouring boiling water through them.

Serve in soups or with dishes that have a good amount of sauce.

Rice Vermicelli

Rice vermicelli has very fine strands and cooks very quickly. Drop into boiling water and cook for 2 or 3 minutes only. Drain well.

Use in soups or braised dishes.

Bean Thread Vermicelli

Also known as cellophane noodles, transparent noodles, bean starch noodles, bean threads, silver threads, spring rain noodles, harusame or fenszu. Cook in boiling water 10 minutes or until tender. Drain.

GLOSSARY

You can find most of these ingredients in Asian stores and many are also sold in supermarkets etc.

ASAFOETIDA   Has an incredible odour. Once cooked its aroma mellows, and it has the reputation of preventing flatulence if added to dried beans and lentil dishes. No more than a peppercorn- or pea-sized piece is needed.

BEAN CURD   Made from soy beans and high in protein. Available in various forms—soft, firm, fried or in tetra packs.

BLACK BEANS   Salted, fermented soy beans, sold in cans or packets. Rinse away excess salt and use as recipe suggests.

CHILLI BEAN SAUCE   Sold in jars, it is very hot and should be used with discretion.

CHILLIES   Handle with care as the volatile oils can cause discomfort to the eyes and skin. Wear gloves when handling. Buy chopped chillies in jars or sambal ulek, a mixture of fresh chillies and salt. Tabasco Pepper Sauce will also add zing. Soak dried chillies before using. Small chillies are hotter than large ones.

COCONUT MILK   Some brands of canned coconut milk are very thick and rich, others extremely thin. Mix the former with at least an equal amount of water; use the latter undiluted.

CORIANDER   Coriander seeds and fresh coriander are different in flavour and usage. Dried ground coriander seeds are one of the main ingredients in curries; fresh coriander herb is an essential ingredient in Thai and Chinese cooking.

CURRY LEAVES (MURRAYA KOENIGII)   Available as fresh curry leaves or you can grow the plant itself. Also sold dried.

FISH SAUCE   A thin, salty sauce used in South-East Asian food much as soy sauce is used in far Eastern food.

FIVE SPICE POWDER   Ground star anise, fennel, cinnamon, cloves and Szechwan pepper.

GALANGAL (ALPINIA GALANGA)   Also known as laos or lengkuas. Similar in size and appearance to ginger. May be bought pickled in brine, which keeps indefinitely in the refrigerator. Also sold as dried slices or powder.

GARAM MASALA   Essential in Indian dishes. Roast separately until fragrant 2 tablespoons coriander seeds, 1 tablespoon cumin seeds, 2 teaspoons whole black peppercorns, 1 teaspoon whole cardamom seeds (remove from pods), 2 cinnamon sticks and 10 whole cloves. Grind as finely as possible and mix in half a nutmeg, finely grated. Store airtight.

GINGER   Fresh ginger root is sold at most greengrocers.

KAFFIR LIME LEAVES   Essential in Thai cooking. Sold fresh, frozen and dried.

KALONJI SEEDS (NIGELLA)   Sometimes called black cummin, although not a member of the cummin family. There is no substitute. Sold mostly in Indian shops.

LAOS   *See* **Galangal**.

LEMON GRASS   Grows easily in Australia. Use the white or pale green portion of the stem, which is tender enough to slice finely. Each stem of lemon grass may be substituted with 2 strips thinly peeled lemon rind.

LEMON SAUCE   A Chinese sauce similar to plum sauce sold in Asian grocery stores.

MAGGI SEASONING   A flavouring which the manufacturers claim contains no added monosodium glutamate. It is given here as a substitute for Golden Mountain Sauce which is similar but contains MSG.

Miso   Miso paste, made from cooked, fermented soy beans, is sold in Asian stores and health food shops.

Mushrooms   Dried Chinese or Japanese mushrooms are the shiitake variety. Dried European mushrooms are no substitute.

Oyster sauce   A thick sauce used in Chinese food.

Palm sugar   Has a distinct flavour but can be substituted with brown sugar.

Panch phora   Combine 2 tablespoons each of black mustard seeds, kalonji (nigella), and cummin seeds and 1 tablespoon each of fenugreek seeds and fennel seeds. Store in an airtight jar. Used to impart wonderful flavour to Indian food.

Preserved radish with chilli   A hot condiment sold in jars, it may be used as a relish or added while cooking.

Rice   Try to obtain the naturally fragrant, long grain varieties basmati or jasmine.

Roti flour   Also called Sharps, the term used by millers to denote the grade to which it is milled. Slightly granular and similar to continental flour, which may be substituted.

Saffron   Try to get true saffron because there are many imitations and nothing else has the same flavour. Expensive, but very little is needed and it keeps well if stored airtight. It is sold in strands (best to buy these) or tiny packets of powder. There is no such thing as cheap saffron.

Sambal ulek (Oelek)   *See* **Chillies**.

Sesame oil   Use oriental sesame oil made from roasted sesame which is dark in colour and very aromatic. Light coloured sesame oil (usually sold in health food stores) will not impart the same flavour.

Shrimp, dried   Popular in South-East Asian cooking, both to simmer whole in soups and also to pulverise to a floss and sprinkle over dishes.

Shrimp paste   Made from dried shrimp, this is used in tiny quantities and is a mainstay of South-East Asian cuisines. Sold in jars or blocks. Keeps indefinitely.

Soy sauce   For best results, use the type specified in the recipe.

Star anise   A dried, star-shaped seed pod which imparts flavour to Chinese food. Simmered in long-cooked dishes.

Szechwan pepper   Small berries that are not hot in the conventional sense, but leave a numbing sensation on the tongue. Only the brown husks provide flavour, so buy the seeded variety. Roast over low heat to bring out aroma, and crush to powder.

Tamarind   Gives acidity to many dishes. It is sold dried, puréed or instant. The dried pulp has the truest flavour.

Tangerine peel   Sold dried, this is a fragrant but expensive item. When tangerines or mandarins are in season, save the peel and dry slowly in a cool oven. Bottle airtight.

Wasabi   Always served (in minute amounts) with raw fish dishes such as sashimi and sushi.

INDEX

green pawpaw 49
grilled eggplant and dried
 shrimp 57
lemon chicken 39
mango 48
onion and coriander 53
seafood 56
Thai chicken, prawn and fruit
 55
Thai dressing 55
vegetables with Nam Prik 58
Sauces
 dipping 13, 78
 Nam Prik 58
Scallops, garlic 29
Seafood 18–31
 simmered, and vegetables 12
 salad 56
Soup
 beef, with salad 7
 chicken and bean curd sour 11
 chicken velvet 1
 Chinese chicken stock 10
 clear, with pork and bean curd
  13
 combination long 9
 hot and sour soup paste 17
 lentil and vegetable 3
 lentil mulligatawny 8
 miso 15
 mixed vegetable 4
 pea, with coconut 5
 pepper water 6
 prawn 14
 simmered seafood and
  vegetables 12
 Thai chicken and noodle 2

with stuffed cucumbers 16
Spices
 hot and sour soup paste 17
 pepper and coriander paste 2
 wasabi 23
Squid, Szechwan-style stir-fried 30

Vegetable
 and lentil soup 3
 mixed, soup 4
 soup with stuffed cucumbers 16
Vegetables
 and braised bean curd 67
 and quick-cooked beef 75
 and simmered seafood 12
 and simmered steak 77
 braised Chinese cabbage 64
 broccoli, Chinese-style 62
 chick peas in spicy tomato
  sauce 63
 crisp greens in oyster sauce 59
 curried pea pods 70
 Indian-style black-eyed beans
  61
 lentil mulligatawny 8
 mixed, with coconut 71
 peas and fresh cheese curry 68
 spicy beans, Indian-style 60
 spicy cauliflower 65
 spicy, diced 69
 stir-fried lettuce 66
 with chicken in oyster sauce 44
 yoghurt with spinach 66
 see also Salad

Wasabi 23